TRADITIONAL COUNTRY
WOODWORKING

TRADITIONAL COUNTRY
WOODWORKING

18 PIECES TO MAKE FOR INSIDE AND OUT

Jack Hill

Photography by James Merrell

MITCHELL BEAZLEY

Traditional Country Woodworking
by Jack Hill

First published in Great Britain in 2005
by Mitchell Beazley, an imprint of
Octopus Publishing Group Ltd,
2–4 Heron Quays, London E14 4JP

The majority of the material and images in
this book has previously been published in
Mitchell Beazley's *Country Woodworker*
by the same author.

ISBN 1 84533 160 5

A CIP record for this book is available
from the British Library

Set in Frutiger

Colour reproduction by Hong Kong
Scanner Arts, Hong Kong
Printed and bound in China by
Toppan Printing Company Limited

Senior Executive Editor Anna Sanderson
Executive Art Editor Christine Keilty
Editor Catherine Emslie
Design DW Design
Production Jane Rogers
Illustrator Julie Douglas, with Jack Hill
Indexer Hilary Bird

Contents

Introduction

It is something of a paradox in the 21st century that so many of the products made in the village workshops of the 18th and 19th centuries throughout Europe and in the early settlements of colonial America, for a population more interested in function than in fashion, are much sought after on account of their bold simplicity and traditional craftsmanship. We may be thankful for the products and amenities of modern technology but we also enjoy the often more satisfying and visually pleasing products of a bygone age.

"Why is this?" we may well ask. Is it because these early makers have come to epitomize a time, and a way of life, when the pace was much slower and less stressful than it is today, or is it because of a growing dissatisfaction with the monotony of urban living and the sameness of

mass production? The idea of the simple country life certainly appeals to many people – a trait that television, magazine publishers, and the advertising business fully exploit with their portrayal of village life, farmhouse interiors, and country living. As a consequence, this obvious step back in time and consciousness has brought about a reverence for and a revival of the handmade products of our rural past.

And nowhere is this more apparent than in the increased interest in handmade wooden objects, be they items of furniture, for use indoors and out, kitchen utensils, or containers, racks, and shelves for storage or display. Traditional woodwork, perhaps more than anything else, is central to the so-called "country style".

From ancient times wood has been one of the most

used of all our natural resources, and throughout history new ways of using it have continually been found. In the beginning, trees provided man's basic needs – food, fuel, and shelter. Later, evermore sophisticated forms of shelter were devised, and buildings (small and grand), and furniture of all kinds to be used in them, were built of wood, as were boats and ships of all sizes, fences and fortifications, agricultural implements, domestic ware, and household utensils. The earliest aeroplanes were made from wood, vintage cars have wooden frames, and giant locomotives on their "iron road" were supported on wooden ties or sleepers. The paper we write on, the pencil we write with, and even the eraser used to correct mistakes began as a tree. The fuels that drive our cars and run our domestic heating come from prehistoric forests that grew

and perished long before man appeared on Earth.

The early workers in wood had only the simplest tools and this is reflected in the simplicity and severely functional nature of what they produced. It is this naivety that appeals to our senses today. The clear step-by-step projects provided in this book, which are organized and colour-coded by an increasing level of ability required for the task, should enable and inspire readers to make their own hand-crafted traditional wooden furniture and artifacts that will help capture the essence of country living and style. Living with wood is undeniably pleasurable and working with it can be deeply satisfying and rewarding.

What You Can Make

Bird House

ABILITY LEVEL
Novice

SIZE
10 x 8 x 6in (254 x 203 x 152mm)

MATERIALS
Pine
Piece of leather or sheet rubber

CUTTING LIST
1 front
10 x 6 x ⅝in (254 x 152 x 16mm)
1 back
10 x 6 x ⅝in (254 x 152 x 16mm)
2 sides
7 x 5 x ⅝in (178 x 127 x 16mm)
1 roof side
7½ x 6 x ⅝in (190 x 152 x 16mm)
1 roof side
7 x 6 x ⅝in (178 x 152 x 16mm)
1 floor
8 x 5 x ⅝in (203 x 127 x 16mm)

NOTE
All pieces can be cut from
a single length, 50 x 6 x ⅝in
(1270 x 152 x 16mm).

A piece of floorboard would
be suitable.

All measurements are given
in inches, with the equivalents in
millimetres indicated in brackets.

Attracting birds into the garden depends on more than just food. Equally important are the other necessities of life, such as water and shelter. Different species of bird have very different nesting requirements, and the box illustrated here is intended to be used by hole-nesting birds such as blue tits, robins, and sparrows. Alternatively, you may find its aesthetic appeal works just as well as part of an interior setting. The size of the hole is critical, since invasion by other species of birds and animals is not uncommon if the recommended dimension is exceeded. With the instructions followed carefully, this project is an excellent starting point for the novice woodworker as birds are not a critical audience.

Method

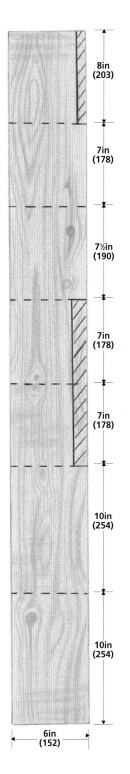

1

8in (203)

7in (178)

7½in (190)

7in (178)

7in (178)

10in (254)

10in (254)

6in (152)

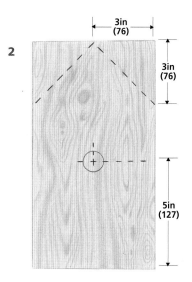

2

3in (76)

3in (76)

5in (127)

2 Mark out the roof line on the front piece and cut away the waste wood to make the required 45° slope. Mark the position of the entrance hole on the front piece and drill it to the recommended diameter, which is 1⅛in (29mm) for small birds such as tits and robins and 1¼in (32mm) for larger birds such as sparrows. If you don't have a drill of the right size, drill a series of small holes and enlarge them with a file. Smooth the edges of the finished hole.

1 Begin by marking out the required pieces and saw to size. Mark each piece for its intended use so that there is no confusion later on.

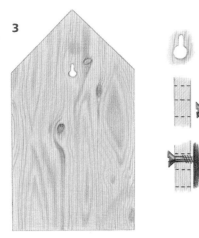

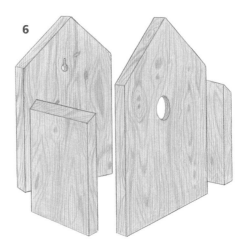

3 Mark out the roof line on the back piece and cut away the waste wood to make the required 45° slope. Make a slotted hole in the back piece for hanging the finished box from a screw or nail.

4 Drill a couple of drainage holes in the floor piece of the box; about ¼in (6mm) in diameter is adequate.

6 Assemble the front, back and side pieces, without glue, and check that the side chamfers align correctly. Adjust as necessary.

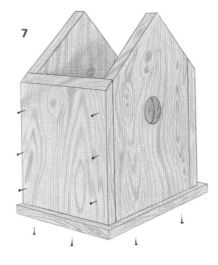

5 Mark out and cut a 45° chamfer on the top edge of each side piece to follow the roof line.

7 Glue and nail the front, back and side pieces together. Use a waterproof (outdoor) glue. Take care when nailing not to split the wood (see page 99 for advice on nailing).

8 Put the floor piece into position. Note that there is an overhang to the front and sides. Glue and nail the floor into place, making sure that the structure remains square. Remove surplus glue and leave to dry.

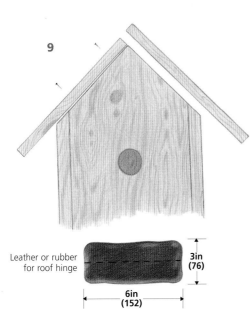

Leather or rubber for roof hinge

3in (76)

6in (152)

9 Check the roof pieces for fit. Note how the longer piece overlaps the shorter. If all is well, glue and nail them into place.

10 Cover the roof joint with a strip of leather or sheet rubber. Attach this securely with large-headed nails or tacks.

11 If you want to be able to open the box for out-of-season cleaning, only fix the shorter half of the roof permanently into position. Leave the other loose with the leather or rubber acting as a hinge.

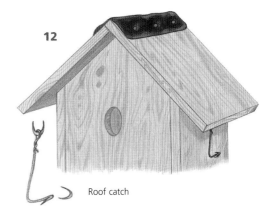

Roof catch

12 Secure the hinged half of the roof with a simple catch. The detail illustration shows how to make this from two small fencing staples and a short piece of wire. Take care not to split the wood with the staples.

13 Perches beneath the entrance hole are not recommended, since they could encourage predators. However, fit one if you like, using a natural twig inserted into a drilled hole.

14 Treat the finished nest box with a suitable preservative, carefully following the manufacturer's instructions and working in a well-ventilated area. Do this well in advance of hanging the box to allow the fumes to disperse. This also applies if you intend to paint the outside.

15 Site the box at least 6ft (2m) above the ground and away from direct sunshine, preferably among trees or shrubs. Put the box out many weeks before the breeding season to allow birds to become accustomed to its presence in their territory.

Five-Board Bench

ABILITY LEVEL
Novice

SIZE
36 x 16⅞ x 12in (914 x 428 x 305mm)

MATERIALS
Pine or any hardwood

CUTTING LIST
1 top
36 x 12 x ⅞in (914 x 305 x 22mm)
2 ends
16 x 10 x ⅞in (406 x 254 x 22mm)
2 sides
30 x 4 x ⅞in (762 x 102 x 22mm)

See template patterns on page 120 for cutting legs.

All measurements are given in inches, with the equivalents in millimetres indicated in brackets.

NOTE
If the bench is to be used in the garden or on a porch, use waterproof glue when assembling the final pieces.

This type of bench was common across Europe and North America, and was most often made in pine and then painted. It was a popular piece of furniture for use both indoors and out. Its attraction lies in the ready availability of the raw material, the fact that it requires little in the way of woodworking skills, and only the simplest of tools are needed. The method of construction means that the bench can be made in an infinite variety of sizes and adapted to fulfil a number of functions. By increasing its height, the bench naturally turns into a small table that, in style, is particularly suited for use in the garden or out on the porch. The dimensions given here are for a generous-sized two-seater.

Method

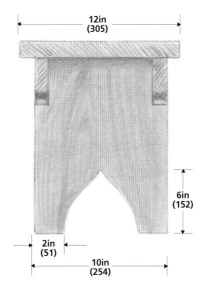

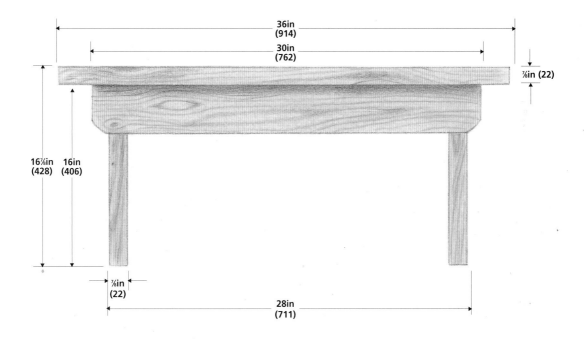

1 Select and prepare all the material using the dimensions given. If necessary, make up the 12in (305mm) width by edge-joining narrower boards (see pages 100–101).

2 Cut out the shapes of the two end pieces (see page 120 for template pattern), or cut them out to a shape of your own design.

3

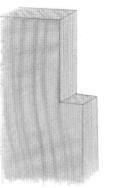

3 Cut the housing for the side rails as shown. Cut these to suit the exact dimensions of the side pieces in case these differ from those given in the cutting list. These housing joints, when well made and glued and nailed or screwed together, add considerably to the rigidity of the finished bench.

4 Now shape the ends of the side rails as shown and smooth off all sawn edges and sharp corners.

5

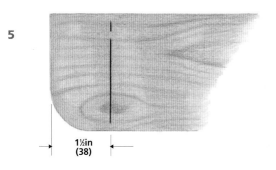

1½in
(38)

5 Mark pencil guide lines 1½in (38mm) in and square across on each end of the side rails as an aid to nailing or screwing. Note the 1in (25mm) overlap over the end pieces. This extra length reduces the risk of splitting when the side rails are joined to the end pieces.

6

4½in
(114)

1½in
(38)

6 Mark pencil guide lines square across the top, 4½in (114mm) in from each end and, parallel to the edge, 1½in (38mm) in from each edge. These, too, are an aid to nailing (or screwing).

7 The bench can be nailed together in traditional fashion, using oval or lost head nails. Take care not to split the wood, especially when fitting the side rails (see page 99 for advice on nails). Punch the nail heads below the surface and fill the indentations.

8 As an alternative, you can join the bench together using countersunk screws. Drill and counterbore the holes to accommodate the screws and the wooden plugs glued in on top to conceal them (see page 100). If hardwood is being used, it must be screwed together.

9

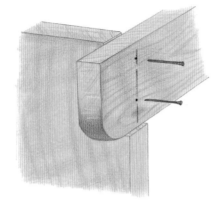

9 Begin assembly by joining the side rails to the end pieces. Apply glue first to strengthen the joints. Nail or screw as required.

10 Check that the basic frame remains square and then wipe off surplus glue and leave it to dry.

11 Check that the top will fit correctly. Line up the pencil guide lines to give about a 4in (102mm) overhang at each end and a 1in (25mm) overhang over each side rail.

12

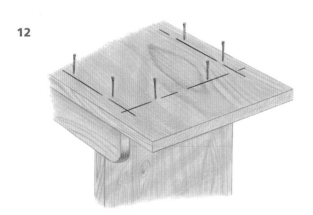

12 Using the pencil lines as a guide, nail or screw the top into both ends and side pieces. The nails or screws will hold better in the side rails than in the end grain of the end pieces.

13 Punch all nail heads below the surface and fill the indentations, or glue and plug the counterbored screw holes.

14 Remove the pencil marks and sand all surfaces clean. Round over all sharp edges, especially those on the top of the seat.

15 Finish according to your choice by clear varnishing, staining, or painting (see pages 108–13 for advice on finishes). If the bench is to be used regularly outdoors the application of a suitable wood preservative will prolong the life of the bench, especially if pine was used in its construction.

Shaker Shelves & Pegboard

SHELVES

ABILITY LEVEL
Novice

SIZE
25 x 22 x 7in (635 x 559 x 178mm)

MATERIALS
Pine, Cherry, Beech

CUTTING LIST
2 sides
22 x 7 x ⅝in (559 x 178 x 16mm)
3 shelves
25 x 7 x ⅝in (635 x 178 x 16mm)

PEGBOARD

ABILITY LEVEL
Novice

SIZE
(Pegs) 5 x 1½ x 1½in (127 x 38 x 38mm)
(Board) 48 x 3½ x ¾in (1219 x 89 x 19mm)

MATERIALS
(Pegs) Cherry, Oak, Maple, Beech
(Board) Pine

CUTTING LIST
(Pegs) 3 pieces 5 x 1½ x 1½in (127 x 38 x 38mm)
(Board) 1 piece 48 x 3½ x ¾in (1219 x 89 x 19mm)

See template pattern on page 123 for side pieces.

All measurements are given in inches, with the equivalents in millimetres indicated in brackets.

The utopian religious movement of the Shakers originated in France but was led in the late-18th century by Ann Lee, from Manchester, England, who emigrated to the United States in 1774. In 1776 she founded the parent Shaker community at Niskayuna, about seven miles from Albany, New York.

Their numbers are now greatly reduced, and the Shakers are best known today for the excellence and simplicity of the work of their craftspeople. Part of the Shaker belief is that work is a form of religious devotion. Within their strict creed – "hands to work and hearts to God" – they create a simple beauty in all they do; functionalism predominates and ornamentation is regarded as

unnecessary "worldly show". Their furniture is plain but always beautifully proportioned. Of their many endeavours, the Shakers are perhaps best known for their fine furniture and wooden artifacts. Many of today's top furniture and interior designers have embraced the purity of Shaker form and style. The simple utility of the hanging set of shelves seen here is typical of their work. Shelves very much like these are made for use in all living and working areas of the Shaker house to hold personal effects, kitchen utensils, and objects pertaining to work. Rooms are also routinely fitted with horizontal pegboards, often in continuous lengths and set at a uniform height, equally used to accommodate all manner of objects, and hanging the shelves (and even furniture) from them is a common Shaker practice.

Shelves Method

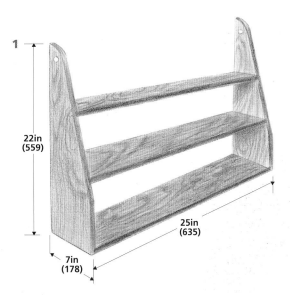

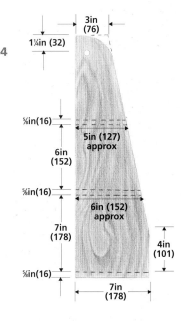

1 Begin by planing the edges of the shelves and gluing pieces to make wider boards if necessary (see pages 100–101). Note that the shelves decrease in width towards the top: the middle shelf is approximately 6in (152mm) wide, while the top shelf is about 5in (127mm) wide.

2 Cut all pieces accurately to length, making sure that they are perfectly square across their ends.

3 Depending on the condition of the wood, plane or sand back all the surfaces so that they are smooth.

4 Cut both side pieces to the correct tapering shape as shown and plane or sand back the sawn edges.

5 Referring to the diagram, mark out the positions of the top and middle shelf housing and the rebate to accommodate the bottom shelf. Carefully check the exact thickness of the shelves before doing this, since all dimensions quoted when buying wood may be nominal only. Make the housing fractionally less than the shelf thickness to ensure a tight fit later on.

Pegboard Method

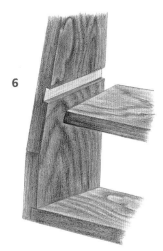

1 Pegs would normally be turned on a lathe (dimensions are given). Simple shapes can be whittled by hand and finished off by filing and sanding. Alternatively, you can purchase ready-made pegs (see Directory of Suppliers pages 124–5).

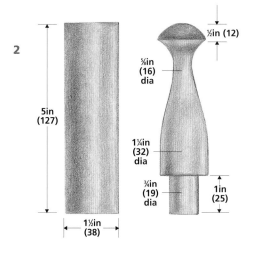

6 Cut the housings and rebate ¼in (6mm) deep and to the full width of the shelf (see pages 100–102 for advice on cutting housings).

7 Check each shelf for fit. If necessary, shave wood from the underside of the shelves.

8 Drill a ¼in (6mm) hole, as shown on page 19, at the top of each side piece for the hanging cords. Before drilling, place a piece of scrap wood under the exit point of the bit to prevent the wood splintering.

9 Assemble the shelves, without using glue, to make sure that everything fits together properly. Disassemble.

10 Glue and assemble the shelves. If necessary, hold them together with cramps and check that all the angles are square. Wipe off any excess glue.

11 The bottom of the rebate joint should be further secured by careful nailing. Take care not to split the wood (see page 99 for advice on nailing). If the other joints fit tightly and are also nailed for security, cramping may not be necessary.

12 The shelves illustrated are made of pine and were later painted (see pages 108–13 for different finishing methods).

2 If turning the pegs on a lathe, place each piece of wood in turn between the centres, or fix each to a chuck and turn to the shape shown – or any other of your choice. Make sure that the tenon joint is true to size and is not too small.

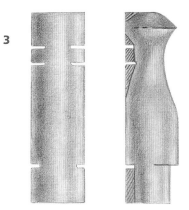

3 If you are shaping the pegs by hand, make preliminary saw cuts all around as shown, and then cut or chisel into these to establish the rough shape of each peg before using files or rasps, followed by abrasives, to refine the shape.

4 Measure the size of the tenons needed in a test hole of the correct diameter, made in a piece of scrap wood.

5 If using ready-made pegs, buy these first and check the diameter of the tenon joints before proceeding to the next stage.

6 Mark the positions of the pegs and drill 1in (25mm) holes (or holes of other sizes to suit) through the board. Drill into a piece of scrap wood underneath to prevent the underside of the board splintering.

7 Try the pegs for size, without using glue.

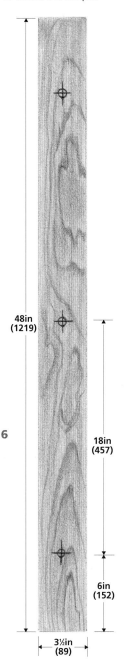

48in
(1219)

6

18in
(457)

6in
(152)

3½in
(89)

8

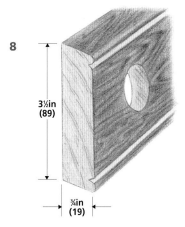

3½in
(89)

¾in
(19)

8 Plane or sand the board smooth. It can be left plain or you can bead its edges using a simple beading tool.

9

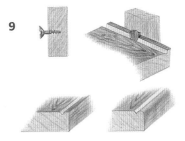

9 As the diagram shows, a beading tool is easy to make out of a screw and a piece of scrap wood. When finished, round off the outer edge with a small plane.

10 Paint the board in your choice of colour; however, keep the paint out of the holes, as this will inhibit glue adhesion.

11 Treat the pegs with a clear finish, avoiding the joint area.

12 When all finishes are dry, glue in the pegs. When the glue is dry, saw off any protruding tenon joint at the back.

13 You can surface-mount the pegboard by screwing it to an existing wall. Countersink the screw heads for a neat finish, and then fill in and paint over them. In new walls, pegboards can be recessed into the plasterwork.

Candle Box

ABILITY LEVEL
Novice/Intermediate

SIZE
18 x 9 x 6½in (457 x 228 x 165mm)

MATERIALS
Pine, Cherry, Oak

CUTTING LIST
1 back
18 x 8 x ½in (457 x 203 x 12mm)
1 front
8 x 8 x ½in (203 x 203 x 12mm)
2 sides
10 x 5 x ½in (254 x 127 x 12mm)
1 bottom
9 x 6½ x ½in (228 x 165 x12mm)

See template patterns on page 120
for shaped and cut-out pieces.

All measurements are given in
inches, with the equivalents in
millimetres indicated in brackets.

Small boxes of all types were once a common feature in country households. They were used to hold all manner of things, from salt and spices to knives, spoons, and, of course, candles, or whatever else needed to be put away safely where it could readily be found. The earliest examples were wall boxes. These were made either to hang from a peg or nail on the wall or designed to sit up against a wall supported on a table or ledge. In their simplest form, these boxes were lidless. However, others did have lids and, as the design developed, further elaboration in the form of the inclusion of drawers took place, until in some instances the formerly simple box became a miniature set of drawers.

Collectors have given names to boxes according to their main use, and in addition to the uses mentioned above there are, among others, bobbin boxes (for storing lacemaking bobbins), dice and domino boxes, and pipe and tobacco boxes.

Some boxes had no specific use, but were merely for keeping safe important documents, letters, personal treasures, or valuable books. These were known as "keeping" boxes. Quite often, they were intricately decorated with paintings or carvings to attest to the value that was placed on them and their contents.

While it may be difficult for us today, with our built-in cupboards, to appreciate just how invaluable these boxes were in the past, they still can serve a useful purpose over and above a decorative one. A candle box makes an ideal letter rack or place to keep the household accounts, while other boxes can be modified to suit all types of modern application.

Method

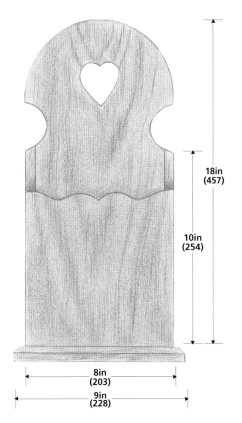

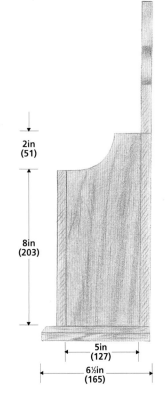

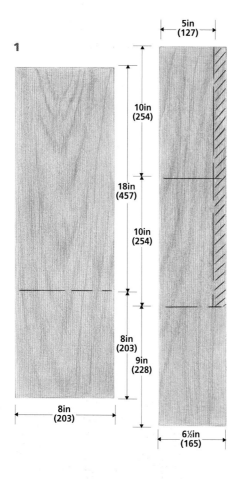

5in
(127)

1

10in
(254)

18in
(457)

10in
(254)

8in
(203)

9in
(228)

8in
(203)

6½in
(165)

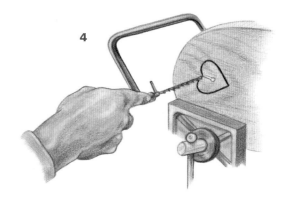

4 For the internal heart shape, first drill through the wood and then enlarge the hole with a fret saw or coping saw. Finish off with a file and glasspaper.

5 Clean off all tool marks on the sawn edges. Check that everything is cut to size and that the side pieces are a matching pair.

6 Assemble the back, front, and side pieces, without using glue. Check the alignment of the matching edges of the shaped pieces. Make any necessary adjustments.

1 Mark out and cut the separate pieces to size. They can be cut economically from two pieces of wood, as shown. Mark each piece for its intended use.

2 Enlarge and trace the template patterns on page 120 and transfer the shapes to the appropriate pieces of wood.

3 Cut the pieces to shape.

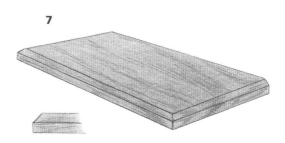

7 Mark out and cut a ¼in (6mm) chamfer on the front and side top edges of the bottom piece of wood.

8 Clean up all the component pieces ready for assembly.

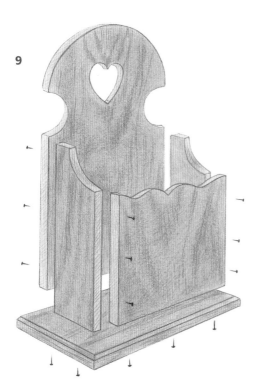

9

9 Glue and nail all the box components together. Use small panel pins or lost-head nails and take care not to split the wood when nailing, especially if you have used a hardwood to make the box (see page 99 for advice on nailing).

10 Begin by fixing the back to the sides, then add the front. Check that everything is square before fixing the bottom in place. Remove any surplus glue and leave to dry thoroughly.

11 Punch the nail heads below the surface and fill the indentations with woodfiller or with a mixture of glue and sawdust.

12 Apply a suitable indoor finish. A traditional beeswax polish will give a warm glow to the wood, especially after a number of applications; varnish will give a tougher, more protective finish. If you want to give your box a well-aged appearance, try one of the special techniques such as distressing the wood, applying an "antique" wood stain, or painting the box and then distressing the paintwork (see pages 108–13 for details).

13 The box can be hung on a wall using two nails, hooks, or small pegs through the heart-shaped cut-out, or you can use a standard mirror plate that screws onto the back of the box. The candle box can also be freestanding and be placed on a table, or perhaps a window ledge.

Milking Stool

ABILITY LEVEL
Novice/Intermediate

SIZE
10 x 10 x 8in (254 x 254 x 203mm)

MATERIALS
(Top) Elm, Oak, Pine
(Legs) Ash, Beech, Maple, Oak

CUTTING LIST
1 top
10 x 10 x 2in (254 x 254 x 51mm)
3 legs
8 x 2 x 2in (203 x 51 x 51mm)

All measurements are given in
inches, with the equivalents in
millimetres indicated in brackets.

For centuries there was no way of milking a cow other than by hand. A milker's stool would be low and sturdy (the example below is relatively tall), with three legs in a tripod arrangement – stable on rough and uneven floors and allowing the sitter to lean forward on two legs, "into" the cow. Even if never used for this purpose, such stools are today collectively known as milking stools. The majority of milking stools have circular seats, although some have a straight front edge. A Scandinavian speciality has only one leg. Today, a milking stool makes a positive contribution to a living room fireside or a country-style kitchen. Children also love them because they don't stand too high.

Method

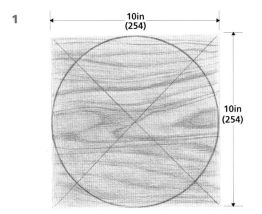

1 Using a pair of compasses, mark out the top piece to a 10in (254mm) diameter circle and cut to shape.

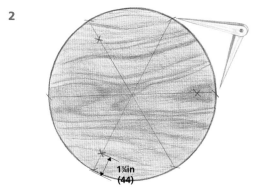

2 Choose the best surface to be the top and, with the compasses still set to give a 5in (127mm) radius, mark off six equal points around the circumference of the top piece. Join these six points with pencil lines and on these mark the three leg positions for drilling, 1¾in (44mm) in from the edge.

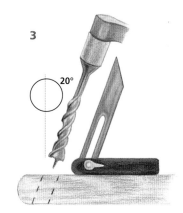

3 These three holes are drilled at a compound angle of 20° from the vertical. This can be done by eye, but only if you are very experienced. There are various techniques to help you get this angle right. A simple way is to use a carpenter's sliding bevel set at 20° as a guide when drilling.

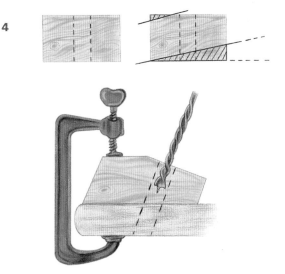

4 However, a more accurate method of working is to construct a pre-drilled guide block, as shown here. When correctly made and cramped to the work, all you need to do is drill into the stool seat through the hole in the guide block.

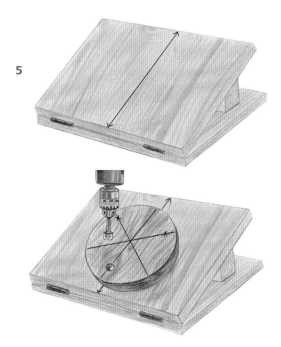

5 Where a pillar drill is available, it is best to tilt the stool top and drill vertically into it. To do this, tilt the stool top up at the prescribed angle by raising one end on a block. Another, more secure, method is to make a tilting-table arrangement, as shown. Use a protractor to measure the angle of the table top, which is fixed by means of a supporting block. By aligning each pencil line on the stool top with a centre reference line drawn on the tilting table, consistently angled holes for the stool legs are assured.

6 Drill three 1in (25mm) diameter holes through the top. A saw-toothed bit is recommended (see pages 96–7 for advice on drills).

7 Clean up the sawn edges of the top and bevel the edges for comfort.

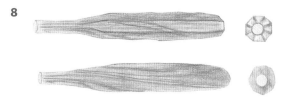

8 Now turn your attention to the stool legs. These can be turned on a lathe, if one is available, using the dimensions given. However, stool legs were frequently shaped using a drawknife or spokeshave, either to a roughly round section or an approximately hexagonal shape. A plane could also be used.

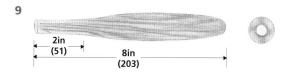

9 No matter which technique is used, the legs must be tapered at the top to form carefully made round tenon joints 1in (25mm) in diameter and about 2in (51mm) in length. This is best done with a spokeshave, but a rasp or file can also be used.

10 Form each joint individually and try it frequently for size in the appropriate socket in the stool top. Bear in mind that although the joint should be a good fit it does not have to be too tight at this stage, since it will be secured later by wedging.

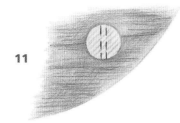

11

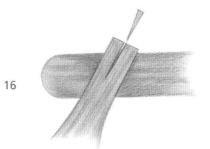

16

11 When all three legs fit, mark pencil lines on their ends to indicate the orientation of the saw cuts needed for the wedges. It is important that the wedges are inserted at right-angles to the grain of the wood of the stool top. Otherwise the force of the wedge could easily split the wood.

12 Remove the legs and make 1¼in (32mm) saw cuts for the wedges.

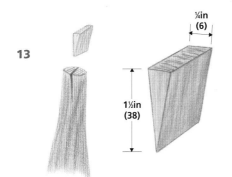

13

¼in
(6)

1½in
(38)

13 Following the dimensions given, make three wedges. Always use a hardwood for the wedges. Make sure that the grain runs down the length of the wedge and not across its width. Try using wood of a contrasting colour to give the wedges an added decorative touch.

14 Clean up all the component pieces. Prepare to assemble the stool by first inserting a little glue into each leg socket. Next, fit the legs so that their tops protrude slightly through the top of the stool.

15 Align each leg so that the wedges will lie at right-angles to the grain of the seat (see step 11 above).

16 Stand the stool upright on a flat, solid surface. Fit the wedges and tap each one part way in using a hammer. Then tap each one again in turn until they are tightly fitting. The weight of a hammer is better for this than a wooden mallet. Check the stability of the stool, wipe off any surplus glue and leave it to dry.

17 When it is dry, saw off the protruding stub ends of the legs and wedges so they are almost flush with the stool seat, taking care not to damage its surface. Clean off the saw marks with a sharp chisel or block plane.

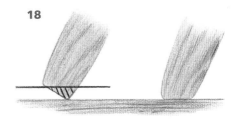

18

18 Saw or rasp off the inside bottom edges of each leg close to the angle made with the floor surface. Then smooth the completed stool with an abrasive paper and apply a suitable finish (see pages 108–13 for advice). Traditionally, milking stools were left unfinished.

Traditional Whirligig

ABILITY LEVEL
Novice/Intermediate

SIZE
20 x 18 x 1½in (508 x 457 x 38mm)

MATERIALS
Wood, waterproof plywood, metal

CUTTING LIST
WOOD
1 platform
16 x 1 x ⅞in (406 x 25 x 22mm)
1 pivot block
3 x 1 x ⅞in (76 x 25 x 22mm)
1 drive shaft block
3 x 1½ x ⅞in (76 x 38 x 22mm)
1 propeller hub
3 x 3 x 1in (76 x 76 x 25mm)
4 pieces dowel
5 x ½in (127 x 12mm) diameter
1 small wooden bead

WATERPROOF PLYWOOD (OR WOOD)
Figure parts, axe, propeller blades, tail, chopping block
24 x 12 x ¼in (610 x 305 x 6mm)

METAL
1 piece threaded rod
5½ x ¼in (140 x 6mm) diameter
6 nuts and washers
¼in (6mm) diameter (to suit rod)
1 large flange washer
¼in x 1½in (6 x 38mm) OD
1 piece brass tubing
5 x 5/16in (127 x 8mm) OD
1 machine screw
2 x 3/16in (51 x 4mm) diameter
1 nut and 4 washers to suit machine screw
1 small screw eye, assorted nails, and screws for assembly
1 piece stiff wire for connecting rod

NOTES
Use waterproof glue for assembly. The threaded rod (drive shaft) should run freely inside the brass tubing. The drive mechanism will need a drop of oil periodically; applying petroleum jelly to the drive shaft before assembly is a useful long-term precaution.

OD = outside diameter

See template patterns on page 122. All measurements are given in inches, with the equivalents in millimetres indicated in brackets.

The easiest definition of a "whirligig" is "a type of wind-driven toy", although spinning tops, beetles, and swivel chairs have also been known by this name. Actuated by all types of mechanisms, and driven by an assortment of different propeller designs, they can be much more complex than the word "toy" suggests. Whether whimsical weather vanes or windpowered wonderments, they are often painted in bright colours. Their objective is entirely non-functional and their intention is simply to entertain and delight. Whirligigs were particularly popular in the USA during the 19th century, and they are now enjoying something of a revival.

Method

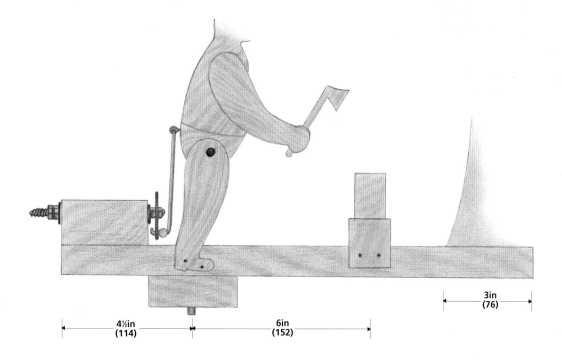

3in
(76)

4½in
(114)

6in
(152)

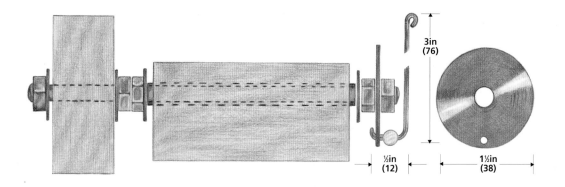

3in
(76)

½in
(12)

1½in
(38)

1 Using the templates on page 122, mark and cut out all of the parts for the figure. Cut one body, two waists, two legs, and two arms. Clean up all sawn edges.

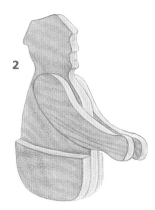

2 Glue the arms and waists to the body, one either side as shown. Cramp the work until the glue is dry.

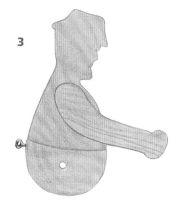

3 When dry, drill the figure pivot hole through to clear the ³⁄₁₆in (4mm) machine screw. Align and drill corresponding holes through the legs at the same time.

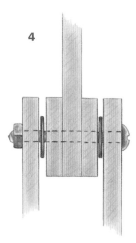

4 Attach the legs to the figure using the machine screw, placing the washers as shown to reduce friction. Check that the movement is free and then put it aside until later.

5 Mark and cut out the remaining plywood/wood components using the templates on page 122. Clean up the sawn edges.

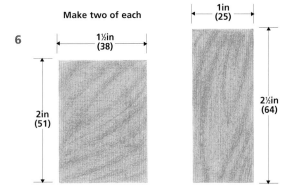

6 From the same material, cut out the chopping block parts and glue these together as shown in the picture for step 14.

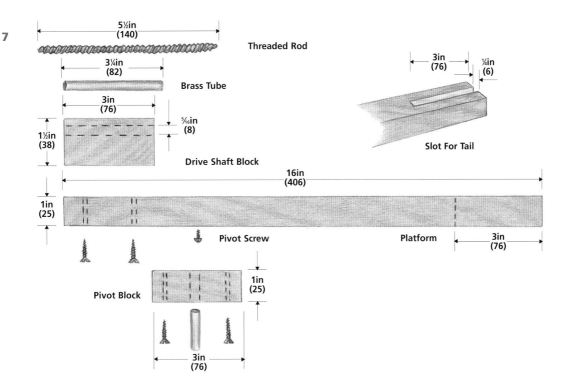

7 Cut the platform, drive shaft block, and pivot block to length. Make a ¼in (6mm) slot in one end of the platform for the tail to be fitted later. Then carefully drill a ⁵⁄₁₆in (8mm) diameter hole through the length of the drive shaft block.

8 Cut a 3¼in (82mm) length of the brass tubing and push this into the hole drilled in the drive shaft block, leaving equal amounts of tubing protruding from each end. File the ends of the tube smooth.

9 Drill a ⅛in (3mm) hole in the outer edge of the large flange washer for the connecting rod attachment. Place the threaded rod through the brass tube and assemble the washers and nuts, large flange washer, and lock nut, as shown. Don't overtighten. Test that the shaft rotates freely.

10 Drill a ⁵⁄₁₆in (8mm) diameter hole through the centre of the pivot block and push the remainder of the brass tubing into the hole to check that it fits.

11 Now screw and glue the two blocks to the platform in the positions shown above and on page 31. In order to reduce friction in the pivot block when it is mounted, position a round-headed screw in the underside of the platform, as shown above, before attaching the pivot block.

12 Glue and nail the figure to the platform in the position indicated. Screw the small eye into the back of the figure at the point shown in the picture for step 3, and then cut and bend the connecting rod wire, using the dimensions given as a guide only. Adjust as necessary. Put the small bead in place; this keeps the connecting rod clear of the end of the drive shaft. Attach the connecting rod to the flange washer and to the figure.

13 Test the movements of the drive shaft and figure and adjust the length of the connecting rod as necessary.

14

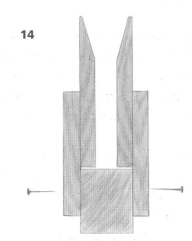

14 Make a deep V-shaped groove in the top of the chopping block and place it in position, without using glue, on the platform. Next, temporarily attach the axe between the figure's hands. Rotate the drive shaft and test the movement of the axe in relation to the chopping block. The axe should go partway into the groove without actually touching it. Adjust the positions of axe and block as necessary and then glue and pin them into place.

15 Make the four-bladed propeller as shown. The correct shape and size of the hub, propeller blades, and other details can be worked out from the templates (see page 122).

16

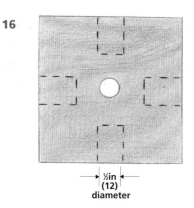

½in
(12)
diameter

16 It is easiest to drill the holes while the hub is still square. Carefully mark and drill right through the wood the ⅝in (8mm) diameter centre hole, and then mark and drill to a depth of ¾in (19mm) the ½in (12mm) diameter propeller arm holes. Either cut the hub to shape or leave it square.

17

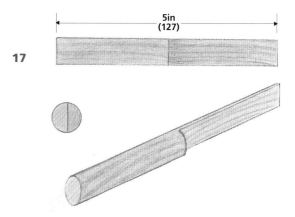

5in
(127)

17 After checking that the arm dowels fit in the holes drilled in the hub, cut the arm dowels halfway through, as shown. The flat surfaces formed by this shaping accommodate the propeller blades. The lower edges of the blades should not be closer than 3in (76mm) to the hub centre.

18 Glue the individual blades into position and secure them with small panel pins, taking care not to split the dowels (see page 99 for advice). Allow the glue to dry before going on to the next step.

19

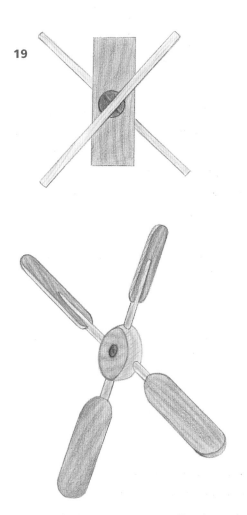

19 Insert the arms into their respective holes in the hub, without using glue. Rotate the arms so that pairs of blades are at opposite angles of about 45° to each other on either side of the hub. Glue the arms into position. Test the propeller for balance, using a spare piece of rod or a suitable-sized nail as a free pivot. If one blade is

heavier, it will always come to rest at the bottom. Remove surplus wood from the blades until the balance is correct. Then fit the propeller to the drive shaft and secure it with the nut and lock nut.

20 Fit, glue, and nail the tail into the tail slot already cut in the platform. The tail piece helps to keep the propeller facing into the wind. When the glue is dry, test the mechanism outside in the wind. It may be necessary to make minor adjustments to ensure smooth running.

21 If the whirligig is to be used outdoors, you must protect it with good-quality oil-based paint over a sound undercoat. You could choose a realistic colour scheme, like the one shown on page 30, which uses earth colours, or go for brighter, more whimsical shades. Make sure no paint is allowed to clog the working parts.

22 When the paint is dry, mount the whirligig on a suitable pivot, such as a steel rod or a nail driven into a stand or post.

23 The drive mechanism of the whirligig will need a drop of oil from time to time to ensure that it continues to work smoothly; applying a light grease (petroleum jelly) to the drive shaft before assembly is a useful long-term precaution.

Spoon Rack & Spoons

SPOON RACK

ABILITY LEVEL
Novice/Intermediate

SIZE
13 x 9 x 5⅝in (330 x 229 x 143mm)

MATERIALS
Pine, Cherry

CUTTING LIST
1 front
8 x 6 x ⅜in (203 x 152 x 10mm)
1 back
8 x 6 x ⅜in (203 x 152 x 10mm)
2 sides
9 x 5⅝ x ⅜in (229 x 143 x 10mm)
2 step fronts
8¾ x 1½ x ⅜in (222 x 38 x 10mm)
3 step tops
9 x 1⅞ x ⅜in (229 x 47 x 10mm)

See template patterns on page 118 for the back and front pieces.

SPOONS

ABILITY LEVEL
Novice/Intermediate

SIZE
10 x 2½ x 1½in (254 x 64 x 38mm)

MATERIALS
Sycamore, Lime, Beech

CUTTING LIST
10 x 2½ x 1½ in (254 x 64 x 38mm)

All measurements are given in inches, with the equivalents in millimetres indicated in brackets.

The simple wooden spoon, one of the earliest kitchen implements, is still used today and it is, in fact, often recommended in order to prevent abrasion that would be caused by the use of a metal spoon. However, wooden spoons sold today are mere shadows of what they once were. Not only are they all standardized and mass-produced, they are also flat and uninteresting. However, antique wooden spoons vary enormously. They are often attractively designed, with deep bowls, perhaps made as decorative gifts, and all made by hand. Spoons would most often be stored in small, open wooden racks on the wall. Here, they would be conveniently on hand as well as a decorative feature.

Spoon Rack Method

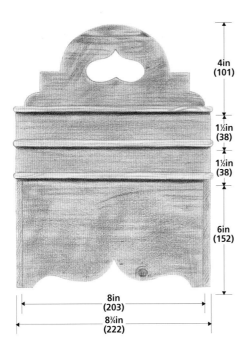

4in
(101)

1½in
(38)

1½in
(38)

6in
(152)

8in
(203)

8¾in
(222)

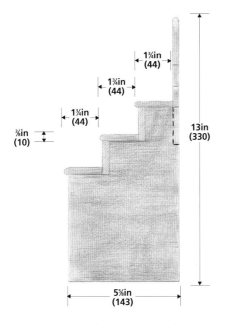

1¾in
(44)

1¾in
(44)

1¾in
(44)

⅜in
(10)

13in
(330)

5⅝in
(143)

1 Mark out the required pieces and cut them to the sizes given.

2 On each of the two side pieces, mark out the "step" shaping. Take care when measuring and marking out to ensure that the separate pieces fit at the assembly stage.

3 Cut each side piece out to the drawn shape. The sawn edges will later be covered, but it is a good idea to clean them up to encourage a good glued fit of the step fronts and tops.

4 Enlarge and trace the template patterns of the back and front pieces (see page 118) and transfer these shapes to the appropriate pieces of wood.

5 Cut these pieces to shape (see page 94 for advice on cutting wood). Cut the internal shape with a coping saw after first drilling through the wood.

6 Clean off all marks and sand smooth.

7

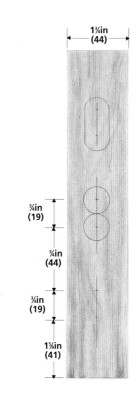

1¾in
(44)

¾in
(19)

¾in
(44)

¾in
(19)

1⅝in
(41)

7 Mark out the three step top pieces as shown, or to any other configuration of holes and slots of your choice.

8 Drill or cut them as required. Drill through into a waste piece of wood to prevent the underside splintering. Sand back any rough edges.

9 Round over or bevel the front edges and ends of each step top.

10 Check that everything fits together correctly and, in particular, that the two step front pieces fit neatly under the overhang of the step tops.

11 Now clean off all surface marks and pencil lines before assembly.

12

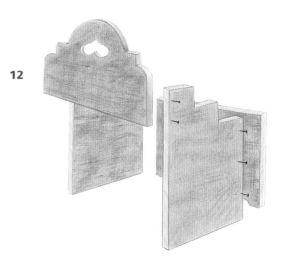

12 Glue and nail the spoon rack together (see pages 99–100 for advice). Begin by assembling the front piece between the two side pieces and then add the back piece.

13

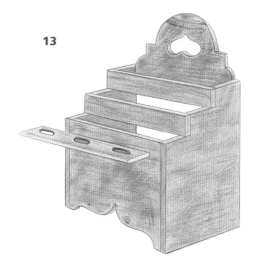

13 Next, put the two step fronts in position and, finally, add the three step tops, beginning at the bottom.

14 Wipe off any surplus glue. Punch all nail heads below the surface and fill the indentations. Leave the piece to dry.

15 Clean up and apply a finish of your choice (see pages 108–13 for options).

Spoons Method

1 Traditionally, wooden spoons were made by splitting a small sycamore log, about 4in (100mm) in diameter, into two halves and then roughly chopping the outside shape with a sharp, short-handled axe.

2

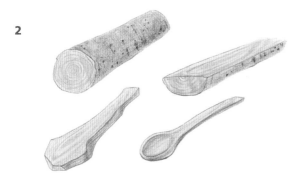

2 After this, the bowl was hollowed out using a special crooked or bent knife. The traditional Welsh carving tool (a *twca cam*) has a short, hooked blade and a straight handle some 18in (457mm) in length. Today, hooked knives, often of Swedish origin, are readily obtainable and can be used successfully instead.

3 Final shaping and finishing was accomplished by means of another small knife and a spokeshave.

4 Spoons today can be shaped by sawing and hollowing out using a curved woodcarver's gouge. The most suitable type is the long, bent gouge designed for scooping out concave shapes. A medium size, medium sweep gouge is best; a ¾in (19mm) No. 6 is fine for the job. However, you must keep the gouge sharp, (see page 98 for advice).

5 In this method the bowl of the spoon is hollowed out first, before the outside is shaped. This allows the work piece to be held safely while the hollowing out takes place.

6

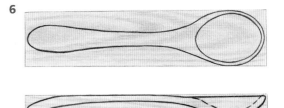

6 Select the material and mark out the shape of your spoon and then cramp the piece securely to a bench in a comfortable working position.

7 Starting at the centre, working outward and concentrically, remove the waste wood. Use a scooping action, going into and out of the material to remove a chip of wood each time. Don't dig in and take care not to go too deep. Aim to get a good finish from a sharp gouge whenever possible.

8 Remove the piece from the cramp and saw the outside to shape (see page 94 for advice).

9 Complete the shaping of the outside by whittling with a knife, or use a rasp and file. Finish off with glasspaper for a smooth appearance, if required. Tool marks can add character if they are left showing.

10 Don't apply any finish. After use, clean spoons by washing and occasional scouring. Never leave a wooden spoon soaking in water for any length of time.

11 Try making some of the alternatives shown in the photograph on page 36. Sometimes handles had simple, carved decoration, and this could be added if you wish.

Scoops & Ladles

ABILITY LEVEL
Novice/Intermediate

SIZE
12 x 6 x 3in (305 x 152 x 76mm)

MATERIALS
Sycamore, Beech, Lime

CUTTING LIST
Flour scoop
10 x 5 x 2½in (254 x 127 x 64mm)
Churn ladle
10 x 6 x 4in (254 x 152 x 101mm)
Ladle with spout
13 x 5 x 3in (330 x 127 x 76mm)

All measurements are given in
inches, with the equivalents in
millimetres indicated in brackets.

Before plastics and stainless steel, wooden scoops and ladles played an important part in the preparation and serving of food and drink. The words are often used synonymously, but scoops are generally broader and flatter, have short handles, and are used for dry goods such as flour, pulses, and herbs, while ladles usually have long handles and are mainly for use with liquids. Spouts, as on jugs, help direct the flow of the liquid more accurately, and hooked handles allow ladles to be hung up, or over the side of a container. The short, large hooked handle on a churn ladle forms a steady support when placed down full on a flat surface. Although usually plain, some were decoratively carved.

Method

3 Early makers were able to use these tools with great skill and little danger to themselves. However, the novice is strongly advised to employ safer methods of working, at least to begin with.

4 More modern methods of working include using sawn pieces of wood, which are marked out in outline and then partially hand- or band-sawn to the required outside shape. The inside shape of the bowl is produced by carving with the workpiece safely cramped to the bench.

Flour scoop (1in/25mm squares)

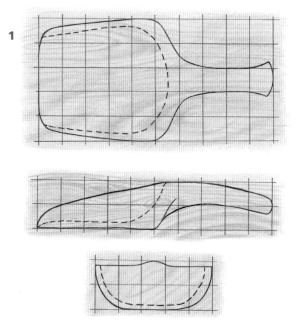

1 Working in the traditional way, a small, often unseasoned log would be selected. This would be split in two and a scoop or ladle chopped out and shaped from each half using a short-handled, very sharp axe.

2 The bowl's inner shape was then hollowed out using a variety of tools, including curved gouges, hooked knives, or – for larger pieces of wood – a small hand adze. The bowl of the scoop or ladle would be completed with a rounded carving gouge or, in some areas (Wales in particular), with a special hooked knife. A curved woodcarver's gouge, of the type known as a long bent gouge, is suitable for this job. The final shaping and finishing of the outside was done with either a short-bladed knife or a drawknife or spokeshave.

1 To make the flour scoop, mark out the shape on the piece of wood by enlarging and using the pattern produced here. First, mark out and saw only to the plan shape. If you are hand sawing, make sure that the piece is held securely in a vice.

2

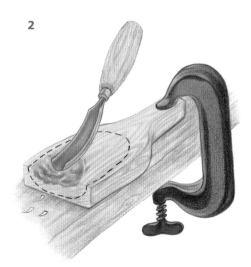

2 With the piece cramped by the handle portion, hollow out the concave scoop with a carving gouge. Begin at the front (open) end of the scoop and work gradually backwards in stages, biting deeper into the wood each time. Finish off using lighter, longer strokes with the gouge to leave the wood as smooth as you can.

3 When you are satisfied with the inside shape and surface, mark in the side view and remove the waste wood down to the lines you have drawn (mainly under the handle). Sawing by hand is best and safest. Complete the outside shape with a spokeshave or use a rasp and file. Next, shape up the handle and bring the front to a firm edge.

4 Finish off the flour scoop by sanding the wood until it is smooth.

Churn ladle (1in/25mm squares)

1

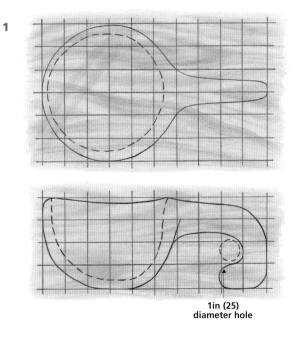

**1in (25)
diameter hole**

1 Because of the generous shape of the churn ladle, you will need a substantial piece of wood. As before, mark out its plan and side views, but do not saw it to shape until after the bowl has been hollowed out.

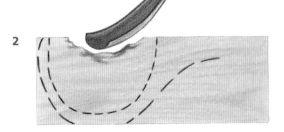

2 Cramp the piece to the bench and, using a carver's gouge, begin at the centre and work outward, more or less concentrically, to remove waste wood from the bowl. Use the gouge with a scooping action, in conjunction with a mallet if it helps you. Don't let the gouge dig in.

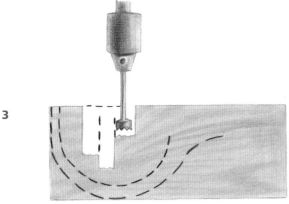

3

3 An alternative is to remove some of the waste wood by drilling it out. Finish off the shaping with a gouge or hooked knife.

4 When the bowl is satisfactory, saw to the drawn plan shape, then draw in the side view. Begin the outside shaping first by drilling through to form the inside of the hooked handle (see 1in/25mm hole in diagram 1). Then hand-saw the waste wood away to the drawn lines.

5 Using tools of your choice, shape the outside of the bowl and handle. Keep the hook of the handle fairly substantial so that it does not break across the end grain, and keep its lower edge flat so that it makes a good support when the ladle is at rest. Finish off by sanding it smooth.

Ladle with spout (1in/25mm squares)

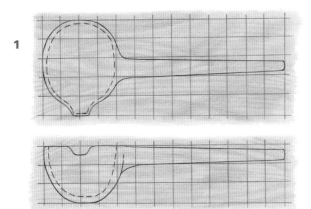

1

1 The ladle with the pouring spout has a shallower bowl and a long, round handle. Making this safely is best done by holding the wood in a vice and working on the bowl first. More experienced woodworkers may prefer to work in the traditional way, whittling with a knife or gouge while holding the wood in the hand.

2 With the plan and side views drawn in, and the piece cramped to the bench, begin by hollowing out the bowl, as described for the churn ladle. Take care in shaping the spout portion and leave it a little oversized at this stage.

3 When you are happy with the shape of the bowl, saw away the waste wood to the drawn plan and side views. Keep the handle full and square at this stage and start shaping the outside of the bowl. Pay particular attention to the shape of the spout to ensure that it pours properly.

4 Finally, form the round handle using a knife, spokeshave, or rasp. Flare the handle out slightly where it joins the bowl to give it extra strength. Finish by sanding it smooth.

5 Like spoons and cutting boards (see pages 39 and 45), scoops and ladles should be left untreated and kept clean by washing and scrubbing them. Never leave them soaking in water for hours at a time.

6 Good work is characterized by good proportions and bowl edges that are strong but not too thick. Final shaping with sharp cutting tools gives a more pleasing texture than a too-smooth finish obtained by sanding.

Cutting Boards

ABILITY LEVEL
Novice/Intermediate

SIZE
12 x 10 x 1in (305 x 254 x 25mm)

MATERIALS
Sycamore, Beech, Maple, Pine

CUTTING LIST
A 12 x 10 x 1in (305 x 254 x 25mm)
B 14 x 8 x 1in (355 x 203 x 25mm)
C 10 x 10 x 1in (254 x 254 x 25mm)

See template patterns on pages
118–19 for handle of board B,
and pattern on board C.

All measurements are given in
inches, with the equivalents in
millimetres indicated in brackets.

The wooden cutting board is still one of the most useful objects in the kitchen today – and they look good too. The advantage of a wooden surface is that it does not blunt the knife as quickly as some other materials, and, contrary to some modern ideas, if properly cleaned after use it is a hygienic surface. Boards come in all shapes and sizes, some with handles and a means by which they can be hung up. For serving bread or cake at the table, circular and sometimes decoratively carved boards are still very popular. Sycamore is the best wood for objects that come into contact with food, with beech and maple close contenders. Pine, although cheap, is too soft and does not wear well with use.

Method

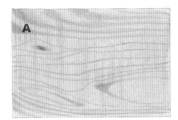

1 Select well-seasoned material wide enough across the grain to match, or at least approximate to, the dimensions given.

2 Where this is not possible, you can make boards up out of narrower pieces edge-joined together (see pages 100–101 for advice on edge joining). Make sure you use a good-quality waterproof adhesive.

3 Plane or sand both surfaces clean and perfectly flat.

4 Where required, draw the outline of the shape directly on to the wood and cut it to shape using any safe method (see page 94 for advice on cutting). Always cut on the outside (the waste side) of the drawn line. The rectangular board (A) is easily marked out using a set square and ruler. The handle of the handled board (B) is marked out and cut to the pattern given on page 119. The circular board (C) is marked out by using a pair of compasses.

5 Clean up the sawn edge surfaces by planing any long straight edges, taking care with the end grain. Use a suitable file or other abrasive tool to clean up curved edges and to get into any awkward corners. Or use a spokeshave. Round over or chamfer the edges so that they are not sharp. Finish off with fine glasspaper.

6 The rectangular cutting board is now complete (see also step 9 below).

7 The handled board requires a ¼in (6mm) hole drilled through the handle to thread a cord for hanging.

8 The circular board has one flat surface decorated with carving. To help you reproduce this design a pattern is given on page 118. You can either trace this off and transfer it to your board, devise a pattern of your own design, or leave the board plain and simply round its edges over.

9 For regular use, the boards should be left untreated with no surface finish at all. Keep them clean by wiping them regularly with a damp cloth and an occasional scrub in water. Traditionally, cutting boards were kept clean by scouring them regularly with wet sand. If a finished surface is required, apply several coats of vegetable oil to the wood.

1½in (38)

Duck Decoy

ABILITY LEVEL
Intermediate

SIZE
11 x 6 x 5in (279 x 152 x 127mm)

MATERIALS
Pine

CUTTING LIST
Body: 1 piece
11 x 5 x 3in (279 x 127 x 76mm) **or**
Body: 2 pieces
11 x 2½ x 3in (279 x 63 x 76mm)
Head
5½ x 2½ x 1½in (140 x 63 x 38mm)
1 dowel
2 x ½in (51 x 12mm) diameter

See template patterns on page 119
for the head and body.

All measurements are given in
inches, with the equivalents in
millimetres indicated in brackets.

Early artificial decoys were native American and were mostly crudely made from bundles of rush covered in real duck skins or simply painted and decorated with feathers, or nothing more than piles of mud and clay and dried grass. A more permanent, floating decoy made from wood then developed, very simply constructed at first, and often blackened by charring or crudely painted. Later decoys became more sophisticated, those from individual makers extolled for their realism and their effectiveness as lures. Today, shooting is still permitted in season and under licence, and decoys are still made, but many are now used only decoratively, and the very best of these have become highly desirable.

Original Method

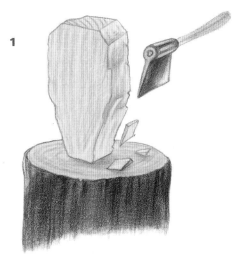

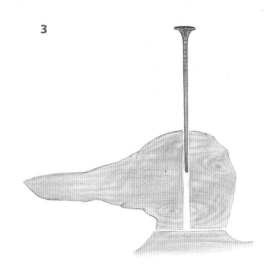

1 In making solid bodies, the early decoy maker would first cut the wood to length and then proceed to chop the block into the rough shape required using a sharp axe. Working at a chopping block of convenient height, he would first remove the corners, roughly round the breast, and then shape the tail.

2 Next, with the roughly shaped body held in a vice, a drawknife or spokeshave was used to refine the shape. An area at the forward end was kept slightly oversize and flat to receive the head. In this process the maker used no patterns or templates, relying only on his skill and experience to achieve the required shape.

3 The head, which demands more careful attention, was sawn to profile according to the species of bird, and then, with the wood held in a vice, it was bored to receive a fixing dowel or nail.

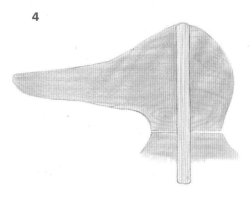

4 The shape of the assembled decoy was then finished off using a spokeshave or by whittling with a knife, and finally sanded smooth before being painted.

Modern Method

 1

1 To make a modern decoy, particularly one intended as an ornament, use the dimensions given and cut the body to size. If you are using two pieces of wood for the body, first glue them together and allow the glue to dry thoroughly before proceeding.

2

2 Using the template patterns given on page 119, begin the preliminary shaping using a saw. If you feel you have the necessary skill, an axe can be used for this.

3 Once you have the basic outline shape, start the detailed shaping using a drawknife or spokeshave, woodcarving tools, or knife. Reference to the cross-sections given in the templates will prove helpful in achieving the required shape (see page 119). For safety, work with the wood in a vice or cramped to the bench during the shaping process.

4

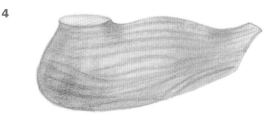

4 Finish off the shaping with a file or knife, remembering to keep the forward area oversize and flat at this stage to accommodate the head.

5 Using the template on page 119, cut the head to shape with a bandsaw or coping saw. Make sure its base is square and flat.

6 Using a blind dowel is the best method of fixing the head to the body of a decorative decoy. For this, drill a ½in (12mm) diameter hole down through the head and fit and glue a piece of dowel in place. In addition to fixing the head, this dowel also provides a convenient grip for holding the wood while you finish the final shaping.

7 Grip the base of the head piece in the vice and shape the main part of the head (using the template pattern and drawn details as a guide). Finish off the detailing and the area around the base of the head, with the dowel already in place held in the vice. Take care not to crush the dowel.

8

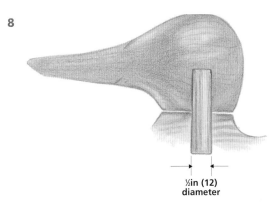

½in (12)
diameter

8 Mark and drill the dowel hole in the body. Lightly plane the flat area left on the body to make a level jointing surface. Try the head for fit, without using glue, and adjust the mating surfaces if necessary until they fit comfortably. Then glue the head to the body and leave it to dry.

9 You can now finish off any of the detailing of the decoy, filing and finally smoothing the surface ready for painting.

10 The paint finishes on early decoys were usually quite dull earth colours, and very little detailing, such as feathers or even eyes, was included. You can emulate this style and keep everything simple, or instead try to produce a more realistic appearance. The body shape and head of the decoy in this project is approximate to that of a male mallard and it may be finished in an appropriate plumage and colours. For reference you could use a colour photograph as a painting guide. See also pages 108–13 for advice on painting and finishing.

Candle Stand

ABILITY LEVEL
Intermediate

SIZE
27 x 13 x 13in (686 x 330 x 330mm)

MATERIALS
Cherry, Oak

CUTTING LIST
1 stem
24 x 2¼ x 2¼in (610 x 57 x 57mm)
1 top
12 x 12 x 1in (305 x 305 x 25mm)
1 brace
10 x 2 x 1in (254 x 51 x 25mm)
2 feet
13½ x 2½ x 2in (343 x 63 x 51mm)
1 dowel
3 x 1in (76 x 25mm) diameter

All measurements are given in
inches, with the equivalents in
millimetres indicated in brackets.

Candles are most often used in some form of candle holder, often a candlestick with a socket just large enough for the base of the candle. When extra height was needed, the candle stand was once a popular choice. They are related to that group of furniture that includes pedestal and tripod tables, and can be highly ornate. However, the stand featured here is entirely utilitarian. It is simple and solid, and is typical of the type used every day in Europe and in the early colonial period in North America. While some designs incorporate a tripod arrangement of "feet" dovetailed into a lathe-turned column, this one features a more easily made, and stronger, cross-lapped-base construction.

Method

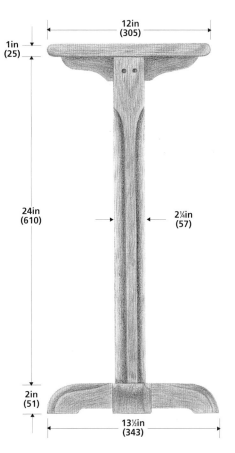

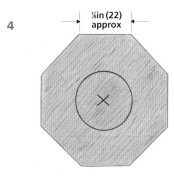

1 If you cannot obtain the top as one piece of wood, you will have to edge-join narrower pieces together (see page 100–101 for advice).

2 Make sure that the top is flat. If you have glued pieces together, wait until the glue is dry, and then plane the surfaces clean and smooth while the wood is still square (it is easier to hold at this stage).

3 Next, cut the top to a 12in (305mm) diameter circle. Clean up the sawn edges and round over or chamfer them slightly, top and bottom.

4 Cut the stem to length, making sure that both ends are square. Mark out the chamfers in pencil as a guide to planing. The finger gauging method on page 93 is accurate enough for this task.

5 Plane the four chamfers to produce the required octagonal shape. Allow the chamfers to taper off, leaving the top 4in (102mm) square for the top lapped, or bridle, joint.

9 Mark out and cut each half of the joint as shown (see also page 104 for guidance). Check for a good, tight fit, make any adjustments that are necessary, and then take the joint apart.

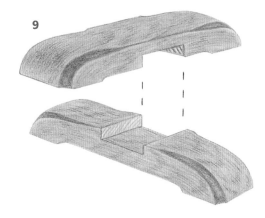

6 Make the bottom joint by drilling into the bottom of the stem, making sure the hole is pefectly straight, and gluing in a piece of 1in (25mm) diameter dowel. This peg joint will fit into a corresponding hole drilled into the assembled feet (see step 12).

7 As an alternative, this round joint can be worked in the solid on the end of the stem. Or a conventional, square, mortise and tenon could be used instead (see pages 104–7). In each case, add an extra 1½in (38mm) to the stem length given.

10 Mark out and cut the scrolled shape of the two feet (as shown in picture 9). Sand back the sawn surfaces and chamfer the top edges.

11 Reassemble the feet to make sure they fit and then glue the joint and cramp the wood together if necessary. Wipe off surplus glue and leave it to dry.

12 When dry, if using the dowel method, drill a 1in (25mm) hole through the centre of the cross lap, again making sure the hole is perfectly straight and in line with the stem. If a mortise and tenon is used, mark out and cut the mortise square through the centre of the cross lap joint. Check this joint for a good, tight fit with the stem dowel. Separate the pieces for the next stage.

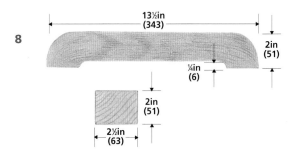

8 Now start making the feet. The two pieces are cross lapped or half lapped so that the top is flush where they cross over.

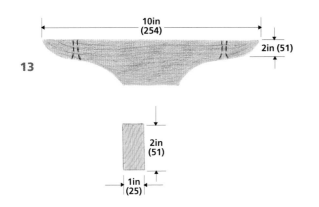

13

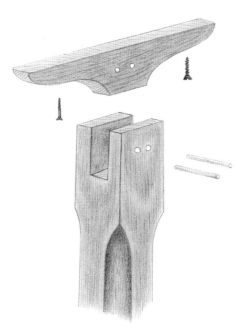

16

13 The brace that supports the top is lapped, full width, into the top of the stem, making what is also known as a bridle joint. Shape and then fit the brace to the underside of the top, as shown. It should lie across the grain of the top piece. Glue and screw it into position.

14 Mark out and carefully cut the housing for the brace on the top of the stem. Take your measurements from the brace itself since they may differ from those given. Check the joint for a good fit; it should not be too tight, since forcing it may split the stem.

15 Disassemble and clean up all the surfaces. When satisfied, glue the stem into the base feet. For extra security, the joint can be wedged (see page 29 for advice).

16 Next, glue the top into place by fitting the brace into its prepared housing. Secure this by drilling two holes through the assembled joint and inserting ¼in (6mm) dowel pegs, as shown. When the glue is dry, either cut these off flush or leave them slightly proud of the surface.

17 Remove any surplus glue and clean up all surfaces.

18 In the past, the candle stand would either have been stained and polished or left its natural colour and given a protective finish using beeswax. A wax finish will bring out the warm colours of the wood, and, over time and many applications, the colour will become richer and deeper. You can achieve this effect more quickly by applying wood stain, and then a coat of wax or perhaps a clear varnish (see pages 108–13 for advice on techniques for finishing).

Rocking Chair

ABILITY LEVEL
Intermediate

SIZE
34 x 16 x 16in (863 x 406 x 406mm)

MATERIALS
Ash, Beech, Maple

CUTTING LIST
2 back uprights
31 x 2 x 1¼in (787 x 51 x 32mm)
2 front legs
14 x 2 x 1¼in (355 x 51 x 32mm)
(Cut the 2 back uprights and 2 front legs from 2 pieces of wood:
31 x 5 x 1¼in/787 x 127 x 32mm)
2 side seat rails
15 x 2 x 1in (380 x 50 x 25mm)
7 stretcher rails
15 x 1⅛ x 1⅛in (381 x 28 x 28mm)
1 back rail
15 x 1½ x 1in (381 x 38 x 25mm)
1 comb (cut from 1 piece)
16 x 4 x 3in (406 x 101 x 76mm)
1 seat (made from 3 pieces)
17 x 4 x 1in (431 x 101 x 25mm)
2 rockers (cut from 1 piece)
30 x 6 x 1½in (762 x 152 x 38mm)

See template patterns on page 123 for comb, seat, rockers, and back uprights.

All measurements given in inches, with the equivalents in millimetres indicated in brackets.

The rocking chair evokes a strong feeling of the past and the comfort of country living. It seems to have appeared throughout Europe and North America towards the end of the 18th century, being most popular in America. The small size of the chair below derives from the fact that from ancient times family life concentrated around the hearth, as the fireplace was the principal source of light and heat. Because the fire was at a low level, so chair seats were correspondingly low. When the table replaced the hearth as the domestic gathering point chairs became taller and bulkier. However, small, hearth-culture chairs as in this project are still found and they are great for children.

Method

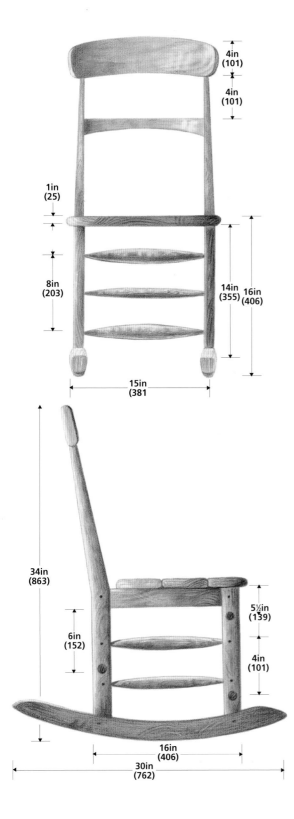

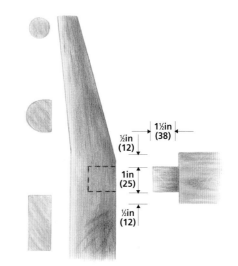

Construction of this chair is simplified if the sequence of making two separate side "units" and then joining these together with cross rails is followed.

1 Cut out the two back uprights (see pattern page 123, c.¼ actual size). Clean up sawn surfaces. Leave rectangular below seat level; above, smooth over the outside edges only and round the top to 1in (25mm) diameter.

2 Make the two front legs and clean up sawn surfaces.

3 Mark out and cut mortises for the side seat rails in the back uprights and front legs (see pages 104–7 for mortise and tenon joint).

4 Check that the side seat rails are of correct and equal length; mark out and cut tenons to fit the mortises. Check for a snug fit.

5

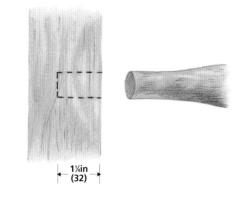

1¼in
(32)

5 Make four round side stretcher rails to length and 1in (25mm) diameter by turning or by any other means. Form ¾in (19mm) diameter tenon joints at each end.

6 Mark the position of the stretcher rails on the inside edges of the front legs and leg portion of the back uprights. Drill these joint sockets ¾in (19mm) diameter and 1¼in (32mm) deep.

7 Test fit the side stretcher rails individually to make sure that they fit properly into the leg sockets.

8 Assemble the dry (unglued) back uprights, front legs, seat rails, and side stretcher rails to make two separate side "units".

9 Cut out a pair of rockers (see pattern on page 123). Clean up sawn surfaces.

10

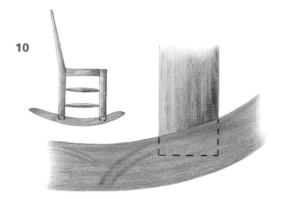

10

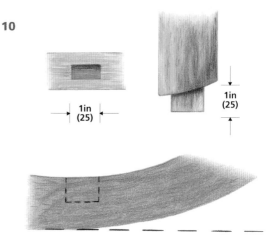

1in
(25)

1in
(25)

10 With the side "units" lying on a flat surface, place a rocker on to each as shown, and mark the top curve of the rocker on the bottom end of each leg. Also mark the position of mortises for leg tenons on each rocker.

11 Cut leg mortises into each rocker. Keep the joint vertical to a flat surface and not to the curved surface.

12 Mark out and cut leg tenons, scribing the shoulder of each joint to the marked line (see step 10) to obtain a close fit with the top surface of the rocker. Check the fit of the tenons into the mortises in the rockers. Disassemble for the next stages.

13

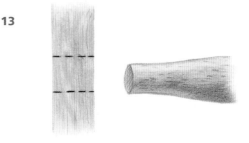

13 Make 3 round cross stretcher rails to length and 1in (25mm) diameter (see page 96 for advice on shaping). Form ¾in (19mm) round tenon joints at each end.

14 Mark out the position of these rails on the outside surfaces of the legs and drill through at ¾in (19mm). Test fit the rails.

15 Mark out the position of the mortises in the back uprights for the back cross rail. Cut these mortises.

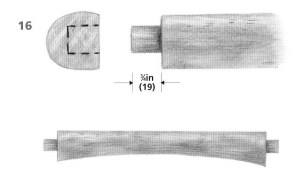

16

¾in (19)

16 Mark out and cut the stub tenons on the ends of the back cross rail. Hollow the front surface of the rail for added comfort, as shown.

17 Cut out the comb to the pattern (see page 123). Clean up sawn surfaces, but to make drilling easier in the next step, leave rounding over the top edge and ends until after the joint sockets have been made.

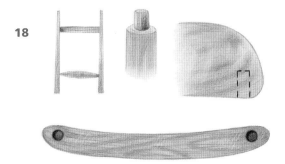

18

18 Temporarily assemble the back uprights and cross rails to check the width apart of the top round tenons.

Mark this measurement on the underside of the comb and drill these joint sockets ¾in (19mm) in diameter and 1in (25mm) deep.

19 Form a ¾in (19mm) shouldered round tenon on top of each back upright and try the comb for a good fit.

20 Make up the seat to the pattern from pieces that may be edge-glued together or left separate. Round over the front edge.

21 To assemble the chair: begin by gluing and assembling the two side "units", including the rockers. Secure the joints by pegging (see page 107).

22 Join the two side "units" together by adding the cross rails. Note that these go through the back uprights and front legs. Secure by pegging and cut joints flush, if they are protruding.

23 Fit the comb on to the back upright tenons.

24 Fit the seat boards by nailing or screwing into the side seat rails. Punch nails or countersink screw below the surface and fill the indentations.

25. The chair may be finished by any of the methods described on pages 108–13.

Rustic Chair

ABILITY LEVEL
Intermediate

SIZE
43 x 20 x 18in (1092 x 508 x 457mm)

MATERIALS
Young growth of Hazel, Birch, or Ash

CUTTING LIST
2 back uprights
43 x 2in (1092 x 51mm) diameter
2 front uprights
28 x 2in (711 x 51mm) diameter
2 back rails
19 x 1½in (483 x 38mm) diameter
2 front rails
19 x 1½in (483 x 38mm) diameter
4 side rails
18 x 1½in (457 x 38mm) diameter
2 arms
22 x 1¾in (559 x 44mm) diameter
1 comb
23 x 1¾in (584 x 44mm) diameter
6 back sticks
24 x 1in (610 x 25mm) diameter
3 "H" pieces
10 x 1in (254 x 25mm) diameter
10 seat pieces
21½ x 1½in (546 x 38mm) diameter

NOTE
Diameters are approximate only
and are given as a guide when
gathering materials. Initially, cut
pieces generously overlength and
allow them to season (dry) before
using them. The ends will probably
split during the drying process.

All measurements are given in
inches, with the equivalents in
millimetres indicated in brackets.

NOTE
If the chair is to be used in the
garden or on the porch, use
waterproof glue when assembling
the final pieces.

Historically, young tree stems derived from coppicing have been used in a variety of ways: fencing, sheep hurdles, fodder racks, and for simple, rustic furniture. In 17th-century North America this furniture really proliferated, and some folk styles today in Eastern Europe, Scandinavia, and the USA still use similar forms of construction. Changes in fashion and the growing pressures of urbanization have led to a revival of interest in the rustic style. Its organic feel, tactile surfaces, and the decorative qualities of the wood and the way it is used have an instant aesthetic appeal and, together with its simplicity, provide the ideal complement to a back-to-nature décor.

Method

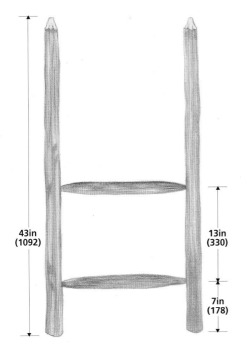

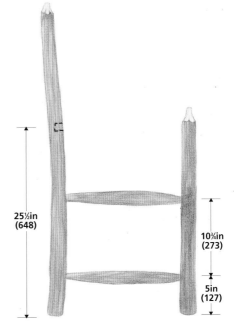

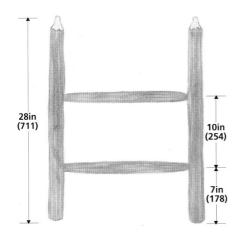

1 Select material according to its length and diameter. Choose back uprights that have a slight backward curve; all other pieces should be as straight as possible. When all pieces are thoroughly seasoned, cut everything to length. Remove the bark if you prefer, using a drawknife. The chair is made in the form of two "ladders", back and front, of different lengths, joined together using side rails. This greatly simplifies the construction process.

2

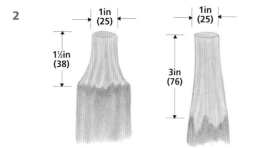

5

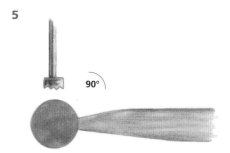

2 First, shape the top ends of both back and front uprights to form round tenons of 1in (25mm) diameter for the back comb and arms, to either shape above. It is important that the top 1¼in (32mm) is kept parallel to ensure a good joint. Use a chisel, abrasives, drawknife or spokeshave to form the tenons.

3 Now mark and drill the joint sockets in the two back uprights to accommodate the two back rails. Do the same in the front uprights for the two front rails. Drill these sockets to a depth and diameter of 1in (25mm). Then shape the ends of the back and front rails to form round tenons, 1in (25mm) in diameter, to fit the drilled sockets.

4 Assemble the front and back "ladders", without using glue, by fitting the rails into the uprights. Make sure the joints go in to their full depth. Mark the component pieces for their correct positions. Disassemble.

5 Mark the positions of the side rails on the back and front uprights and drill these to a depth and diameter of 1in (25mm), and at right angles to those previously drilled.

6

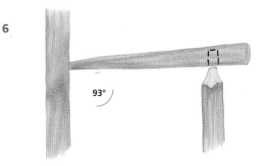

6 Now mark and drill the sockets to hold the arms. These angle slightly upward, as shown, to allow for the slope of the arms. Next, shape the ends of the side rails (see step 3) to form 1in (25mm) diameter tenons. Test fit rails in their respective sockets, making sure they enter to their full depth.

7 Reassemble the front and back "ladders", without gluing. Join these to the side rails to make the basic chair frame. Check that the chair stands without rocking. If necessary, use a soft mallet to tap the joints fully home.

8 Now mark the positions of the other components in the following order, although the measurements given are only a guide and may differ from chair to chair.

9

87°

9 First, shape the joint end of each of the arms to a diameter of 1in (25mm) and fit them into their previously drilled sockets in the back uprights. Make sure they enter to their full depth and, while they are in place, mark the positions for drilling the front arm sockets to fit the tenons already made on the top of each front upright. Next, drill the arms at the marked positions to a depth and diameter of 1in (25mm) and test fit the components. Drill these sockets at a slight angle to allow for the slope of the arms. Round over or bevel the front end of each arm.

10 Mark the position of the sockets in the back comb to fit the tenons on the top of each back upright. Drill these to a depth and diameter of 1in (25mm) and test fit the components. Round over or bevel the ends. Note that the back comb drops down onto the back upright tenons. This facilitates the fitting of the six back sticks

11

18½in
(470)

2½in
(64)
approx

11 Mark the positions of the sockets for the six back sticks on the top surface of the back rail and the underside of the back comb. Space these out equally, about 2½in (64mm) apart, but check this on your own chair.

12 Mark the position of the vertical pieces of the front "H" on the top and bottom front rails, at the places shown. Disassemble basic frame. Drill back stick sockets to a diameter of ⅝in (16mm) and a depth of ¾in (19mm).

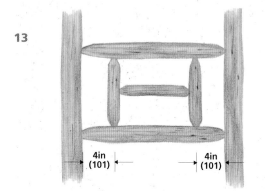

13

4in (101)   4in (101)

13 Drill the front "H" sockets in the top and bottom front rails, to a diameter of ⅝in (16mm) and a depth of ¾in (19mm). Also drill the sockets for the cross piece.

14 Shape the ends of the back sticks to form ⅝in (16mm) diameter round tenons. Test these in turn for fit in the drilled sockets. Then assemble the entire back "ladder", without gluing. Check for fit and square.

15 Shape the ends of the "H" pieces and try them individually for fit in the previously drilled sockets. Some adjustment of length may be needed. Without gluing, fit the front "H" into the front rails, assemble the entire front "ladder", and check for fit and square.

16 Without gluing, join the front and back "ladders" together with the side rails and put the arms into position. Check the complete chair goes together properly, then disassemble ready for gluing. First, glue together the back "ladder" and the front "ladder". Check that all joints fit to their full depth and that all is square. Add the side rails, then the arms. Make sure the

joints fit to their full depth. Check the assembled chair stands upright on a level surface. You may want to peg the arms and the top front and top side rails (see page 107) for extra strength.

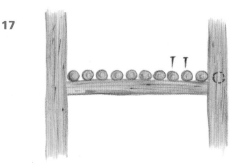

17

17 The seat consists of several separate pieces placed side by side across the side seat rails, their tops level with the top front rail. Nail these into place, using a single oval or lost head nail at each end. To avoid splitting the wood, drill a small hole in each piece first, then punch the nail heads below the surface.

18 Give the completed chair an oil finish or treat it with two or three coats of thinned polyurethane varnish. The use of a suitable wood preservative is recommended (see pages 108–13 for advice on finishes).

Hooded Cradle

ABILITY LEVEL
Intermediate

SIZE
34 x 17 x 20in (864 x 432 x 508mm)

MATERIALS
Pine, Cherry, Oak

CUTTING LIST
2 sides
34 x 14 x ¾in (864 x 356 x 19mm)
1 top end
17 x 14 x ¾in (432 x 356 x 19mm)
1 lower end
15½ x 12½ x ¾in (394 x 317 x 19mm)
1 bottom
27½ x 12½ x ½in (699 x 317 x 12mm)
2 hood sides
11 x 6 x ¾in (279 x 152 x 19mm)
1 hood back
17 x 6 x ¾in (432 x 152 x 19mm)
1 hood arch
17 x 4 x ¾in (432 x 101 x 19mm)
1 hood top
14 x 10 x ½in (356 x 254 x 12mm)
2 rockers
24 x 4 x 1in (610 x 101 x 25mm)
1 brace
27 x 2 x ¾in (686 x 51 x 19mm)

See template patterns on page 121 for cradle rocker and hood arch.

All measurements are given in inches, with the equivalents in millimetres indicated in brackets.

Many cradles become cherished objects, even family heirlooms. The very earliest types were woven baskets, and later they were simple open boxes swung between two uprights. Then, cradles mounted on rockers and placed on the floor came into common use, and this basic design has remained popular ever since. Oak was the usual choice, but beech, elm, and various fruitwoods were sometimes used. Extra detail might include knobs or finials, carvings, and decorative wood inlay. Simpler cradles like the one here had solid-boarded sides and ends and were of different depths depending on the climate. Hoods provided extra protection and were often hinged for easy access.

Method

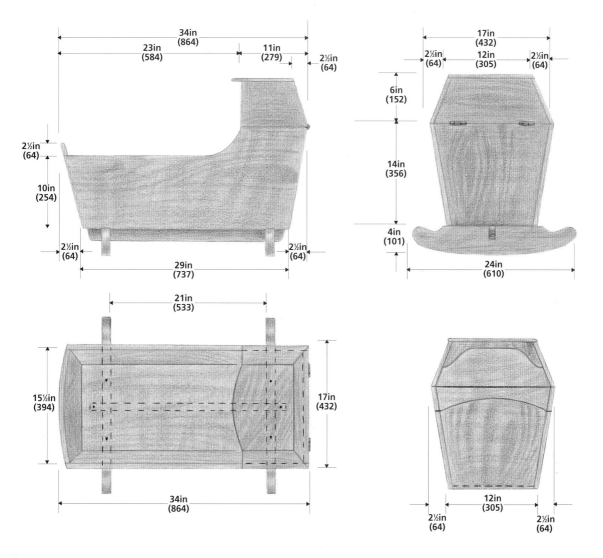

1 Make the body of the cradle first. Use wide boards if possible or edge-join narrow boards to make the required widths (see pages 100–101).

2 Mark out and cut the side pieces, as shown, and clean up the sawn edges.

3 Mark out and cut the two end pieces and clean up the sawn edges.

4 The sides are joined to the ends using glue and either nails or screws – screws are preferred. If nails are used they should be 1½in (38mm) lost head or oval nails, knocked in dovetail fashion for extra security (see page 99).

5 To use screws, drill and counter-bore the side pieces (see page 100).

6 Screw the sides and ends together without glue to check that they fit correctly, then disassemble for the next stage.

7 Apply glue to the joint areas and join the sides and ends of the cradle. Wipe off surplus glue, check the cradle body is square and leave the glue to dry. Plug the screw holes and clean off flush, or punch nails below the surface and fill.

8

8 Prepare the cradle bottom. Cut this oversize to the inside measurements across the bottom of the cradle initially. Then, fitting from the top, trim it to a bevel edge all around to obtain a wedge fit, flush with the bottom edges of the cradle body.

9 When this is achieved, glue and panel pin the bottom into position and leave it until the glue is dry.

10 When the glue is dry, trim the joined edges of the cradle body flush and round over any sharp corners.

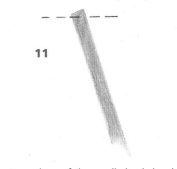

11

11 Plane the top edges of the cradle body level where the hood will fit.

12 Now make the hood. The dimensions in the cutting list are only a guide; use the actual measurements taken from your cradle, since they may differ slightly.

13 Mark out and cut the back piece first to establish the shape of the hood. From these same outside dimensions, mark out and cut the arch piece.

14 Cut the inside shape of the arch piece and round over its inside edge (see template pattern on page 121).

15 Mark out and then carefully cut the two side pieces.

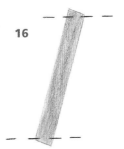

16

16 Bevel the top and bottom edges of the back and side hood components to improve the contact with the cradle body and with the flat top, when it is fitted. Do this with a plane and don't worry if mating bevels are not perfect.

17 Holding them temporarily together, check that the hood back and sides fit and match up correctly on the cradle body. Adjust if necessary; take care not to make the hood components too small.

18 Glue and nail (or screw) the hood components together. Check that the shape of the hood still fits the cradle body and that it is square. Wipe off surplus glue and leave it to dry. Plug the screw holes and clean off flush or conceal nails.

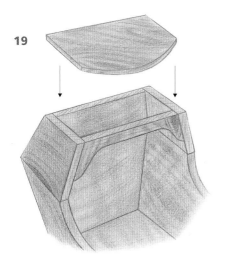

19

19 Cut to size and fit the flat top. Glue and panel pins are sufficient, but avoid splitting the wood (see page 99).

20 Clean up the completed hood by planing joined edges flush and rounding over any sharp corners.

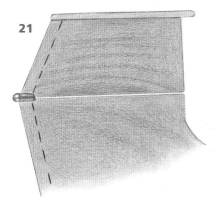

21

21 The hood is hinged to the cradle body (see page 82 for advice on hinges).

22 Now make and fit the rockers. Cut out the two rockers (see template on page 121) and clean up the sawn edges. Round over the rocking edges so that they don't become "carpet cutters". Cut out for the half lap joint with the centre brace (see page 104).

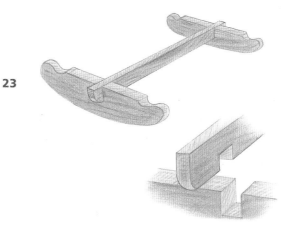

23

23 Cut the centre brace to size and shape and clean up the sawn edges. Cut out for the half lap joints with rockers.

24 Try the half lap joints for fit and adjust them if necessary.

25 Stand the cradle on the rockers/brace assembly and measure and mark its position on the inside of the cradle bottom.

26 Drill and countersink two holes along the line of each rocker and two holes (you could use three to be sure) along the line of the brace, as shown in picture 27 and the plan view on page 65.

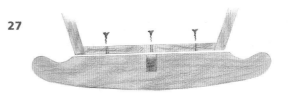

27

27 Fit the rockers and brace in position with screws through the bottom of the cradle.

28 Round over any remaining sharp edges and sand everything to a smooth finish. Apply a suitable, non-toxic stain and polish or paint the cradle as required (see pages 108–13 for advice on finishing methods).

Blanket Box

ABILITY LEVEL
Intermediate/Experienced

SIZE
40 x 18 x 19in (1016 x 457 x 483mm)

MATERIALS
Pine, Cedar

CUTTING LIST
2 sides
40 x 17½ x ⅞in (1016 x 445 x 22mm)
2 ends
18 x 17½ x ⅞in (457 x 445 x 22mm)
1 top
42 x 18 x ⅞in (1067 x 457 x 22mm)
1 bottom
40 x 18 x ⅞in (1016 x 457 x 22mm)
4 end battens
18 x 2 x ⅞in (457 x 51 x 22mm)
3 long battens
40 x 2 x ⅞in (1016 x 51 x 22mm)
1 centre batten
17 x 3 x ⅞in (432 x 76 x 22mm)
Pair "T" hinges
Brass box lock with brass plate
4 x 4in (101 x 101mm)

All measurements are given in
inches, with the equivalents in
millimetres indicated in brackets.

A chest, in addition to holding clothing, bed linen, and valuables, also served as seat, table, and sometimes bed in the homes of our ancestors. The most primitive were little more than hollowed-out tree trunks, then rough-hewn oak boards joined at their corners with wrought iron nails and iron straps. In the late-14th century vertical end pieces known as stiles were introduced on many chests, while others had crude dovetailed joints. As techniques developed, frame and panel construction came into use and dovetail joints improved. Chests thus became lighter in weight, and economical in terms of materials and the skills required to make them. This multi-purpose item remains popular today.

Method

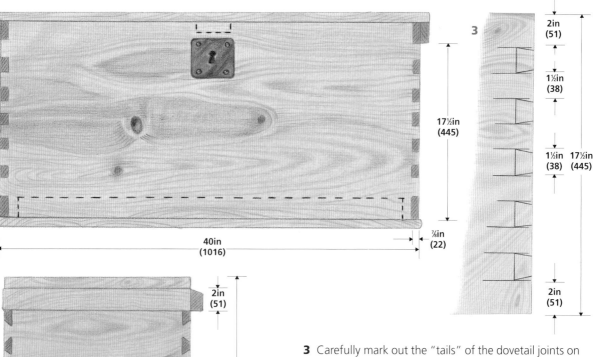

3 Carefully mark out the "tails" of the dovetail joints on the end pieces (see page 103) using the measurements given. Note: top and bottom tails are the largest at 2in (51mm); all the others are equal divisions of 1½in (38mm). Cut out the "tails".

4 Using the "tails" as a template, mark out and cut the "pins" or sockets (see page 103).

5 Test fit the mating dovetails, but not too often as this loosens the joint, and adjust as necessary.

6 Prepare for assembly by cleaning off surface marks and guide lines from the sides and ends, inside and out. Have cramps ready to hand, but if the joints are tight fitting these may not be necessary.

7 Glue up the sides and ends to make the main carcass. Cramp up, if required, and check that the work is square. Wipe off surplus glue and leave it to dry.

1 Ideally this project should be made, as the original (left) was, from single wide boards. If you can't locate suitable boards, you will have to edge-join narrower ones to make up the required widths (see pages 100–101 for advice).

2 Cut the two long sides and two end pieces to the correct width and length and make sure the ends are square. Select the face sides and keep these facing outward. Leave the top and bottom pieces a little oversize at this stage; these will be trimmed to fit after the side and end pieces are assembled to make the main carcass.

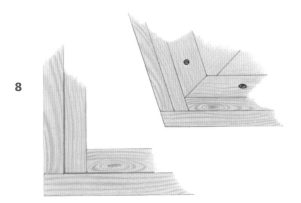

8 Cut to the correct size two of the end battens and two of the long battens and fit them to the inside of the carcass, flush with the bottom edge. Glue and screw, or nail, the battens into place.

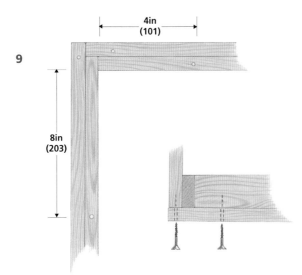

9 Trim the bottom to fit the outside dimensions of the carcass. Secure it in place with countersunk screws, staggering them at about 4in (101mm) intervals on the ends, and at 8in (203mm) intervals along the sides.

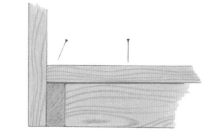

10 This method of fitting the bottom is true to the original rather than being the best technique. A better method is to trim the bottom to fit inside the carcass so that it rests on the battens fitted on the inside.

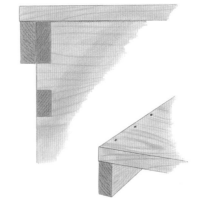

11 Now cut the top to size. It should match the outside dimensions across the width of the carcass but overhang the two end battens (when fitted) so that it does not interfere with the ends of the carcass when the lid is closed (see detail).

12 Cut the two end battens to size and fit them to the top, as shown, by gluing and screwing, or nailing. Clean up the sawn edges and smooth over the sharp corners.

13 Cut the centre batten (3in/76mm) to fit, without interference, the inside dimension across the width of the carcass. Fit this square across the inside surface of the top. Use glue and screws for the strength needed when the lock is fitted.

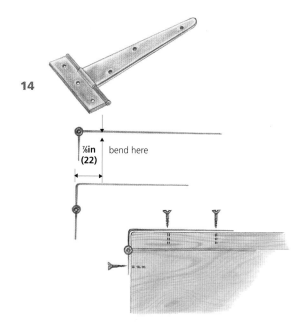

14 The original chest had long, cranked hinges to secure the top to the carcass. These are now difficult to obtain, but you can use modern "T" hinges instead. Modify these by carefully bending them, as shown, or use ordinary butt hinges instead (see page 82, step 20, for advice on fitting hinges).

15 Make sure that the top closes without straining the hinges. Some adjustment may be required.

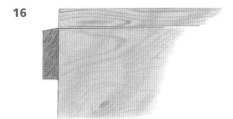

16 Fix the remaining long batten to the back of the box – flush with the top edge – using glue and screws, or nails. Lightly chamfer the top edge of the batten away from the carcass before fitting, and cut away some of the wood at the hinge positions. When fitted, this batten prevents the top swinging back too far when opened.

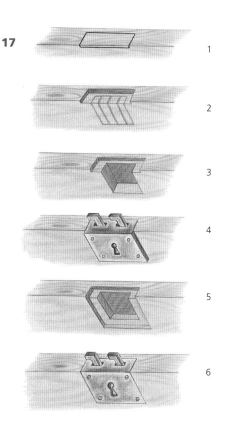

17 Follow the illustrations here for fitting a heavy-duty lock to the box. Locate its position and drill through for the key hole. Then, on the inside, chisel out a recess to accommodate the body of the lock. The catch plate, which is supplied with the lock, is attached to the underside of the top, close to the centre batten.

18 After fitting the lock, a brass plate measuring 4 x 4in (101 x 101mm) with a suitable key hole can be screwed to the outside, to imitate the original lock plate.

19 When everything is complete, clean off all surface marks and smooth any rough edges, and then apply the finish of your choice. The original had a stained finish, details of which are on page 108–11. If you have used cedar, leave the inside untreated since the odour of the wood deters moths.

Side Table

ABILITY LEVEL
Experienced

SIZE
36 x 30 x 22in (914 x 762 x 559mm)

MATERIALS
(Top) Pine
(Frame) Oak, Cherry, Beech

CUTTING LIST
1 top
36 x 22 x ⅞in (914 x 559 x 22mm)
4 legs
28 x 2½ x 2½in (711 x 63 x 63mm)
2 side rails
27½ x 5 x ⅞in (699 x 127 x 22mm)
2 end rails
13½ x 5 x ⅞in (343 x 127 x 22mm)
2 cross rails
14 x 2 x ⅞in (356 x 51 x 22mm)
2 drawer runners
13 x ⅞ x ⅞in (330 x 22 x 22mm)
1 drawer front
16 x 3½ x ⅞in (406 x 89 x 22mm)
2 drawer sides
12 x 3½ x ½in (305 x 89 x 12mm)
1 drawer back
16 x 3 x ½in (406 x 76 x 12mm)
1 drawer bottom
13 x 16 x ¼in (330 x 406 x 6mm)

All measurements are given in inches, with the equivalents in millimetres indicated in brackets.

The side table is a frequently-seen table design, which was first developed in the early 17th century. It usually has a square or rectangular top, though some are semicircular. In earlier times pairs were often made to stand at each end of a formal dining area. A table such as the one in this project should be placed to one side, as the name suggests, against a wall, where it might function as a writing table – a drawer being especially useful in this role. In the past tables of this kind were generally made of a hardwood frame for strength, with an inexpensive top constructed out of softwood, such as pine, and stained to match. For kitchen use leave the top unstained and keep clean by scrubbing.

Method

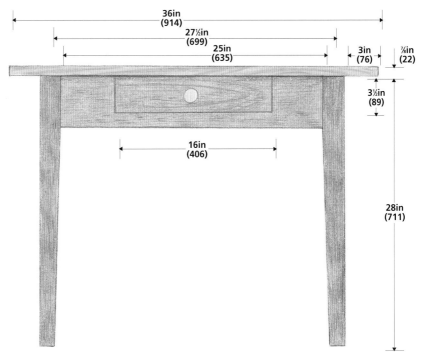

36in
(914)

27½in
(699)

25in
(635)

3in
(76)

⅞in
(22)

3½in
(89)

16in
(406)

28in
(711)

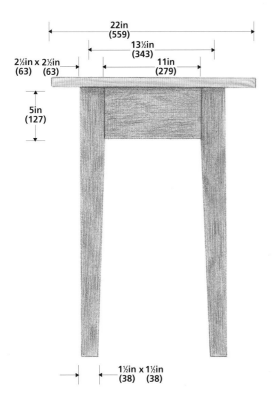

22in
(559)

13½in
(343)

11in
(279)

2½in x 2½in
(63)   (63)

5in
(127)

1½in x 1½in
(38)   (38)

1 The top is made by edge-joining narrower boards. Begin by selecting straight pieces of pine, planing their mating edges and joining them using the simple "rubbed joint", or an alternative method described on pages 100–101. If the top is to be left untreated for kitchen use, apply a waterproof glue.

2 Glue up the top. Check that it is flat, apply glue to the mating edges and use a minimum of three cramps as shown and described on page 101.

3 Cut the frame materials to size. The legs are tapered and the frame is fixed together with double mortise and tenon joints (see page 106 for advice on this joint).

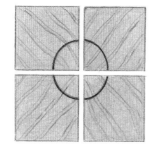

4 Mark the top ends of the legs in pencil as shown above. This is a useful guide in identifying inside surfaces for tapering (step 5), and adjacent surfaces for the mortise positions (step 6) as shown in diagram 7.

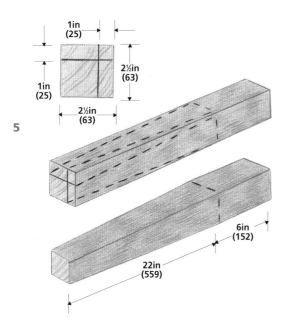

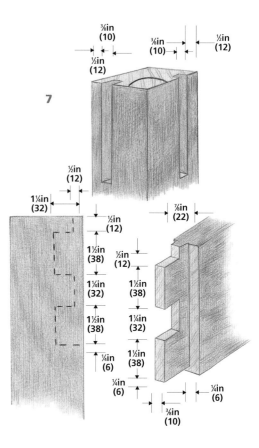

5 Taper the legs on two inside surfaces only, leaving the top 6in (152mm) of the legs untapered. Remove the bulk of the waste wood by sawing followed by hand planing. Sand the edges to remove the sharp edges.

6 Mark out the double mortise positions on the legs. Cut the mortises, keeping them straight and square. Note the recesses for the tenon haunch and central tongue.

7 Mark out the double tenons as shown on the side and end rails. Cut the tenons straight and square. Remember the haunch and central tongue (see page 106).

8 Test fit the tenons into their respective mortises. Trim as required for a good fit.

9 Assemble the legs and the side and end rails, without using glue, and check that everything fits well and is square.

10 Check the position of the cut-out for the drawer and the position and required length (including the stub tenons) of the two internal cross rails, which support and strengthen the frame. Disassemble.

11 Mark out and cut the drawer opening on the front side rail. This opening should finish at 16in x 3½in (406 x 89mm).

12 Mark the position of the mortises for the cross rails on the inside surfaces of the side rails (see illustration below). Ensure that the cross rails will be parallel. Cut the mortises carefully, no more than ½in (12mm) deep.

13 Mark out the stub tenons on the cross rails. Cut these and check them individually for a good fit. The cross rails should be just flush with the drawer opening.

14 Trial assemble the complete frame, including the cross rails, which must be put in position first. Disassemble.

15 If the leg joints are to be additionally secured with wooden pins, these should be prepared now (see page 107 for "draw boring"). Clean off all surface marks and prepare for gluing.

16 Glue and assemble the complete frame. Fit the cross rails first, then join the rails to the legs. Hold them with cramps or insert securing pegs. Check that the frame is square, clean off surplus glue, and leave until the glue has completely dried.

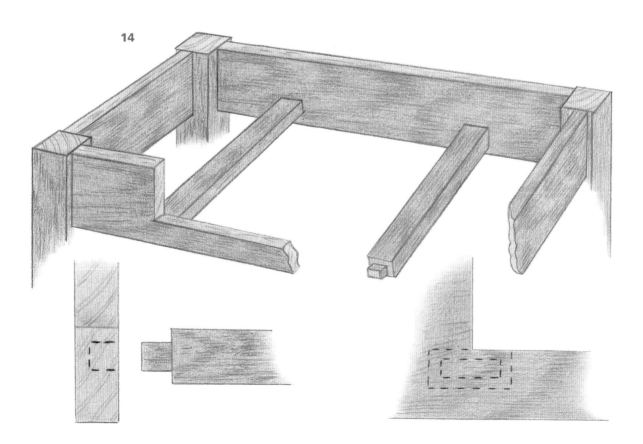

14

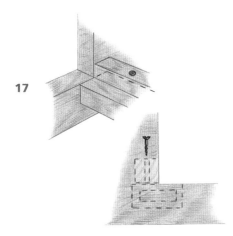

17

17 Prepare and fit the drawer runners. Screw these into place rather than gluing them. They should be just flush with the drawer opening and parallel to each other.

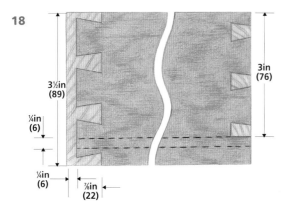

18

3½in (89)

3in (76)

¼in (6)

¼in (6)

⅞in (22)

18 Now make the drawer. First, plane the drawer front to be a tight fit in the drawer opening. Cut the two drawer side pieces to exactly the same width (drawer height) as the drawer front and check that the adjoining ends are square. Cut the drawer back piece to the same length as the drawer front, but note that it is narrower than the front and side pieces; this allows the drawer bottom to pass underneath.

19 Cut the groove to accommodate the drawer bottom in the front and side pieces. (See the markings in the diagram above.)

20 Mark out and cut the dovetail joints: lapped joints at the front and through joints at the back. See pages 102–3 for method, and diagram 18 on this page.

21 First mark and cut the "tails" on each end of the side pieces. Then mark and cut the "sockets" on the front and back pieces respectively, using the "tails" already cut as a template in each case.

22 Test fit each joint, as little as possible, and adjust as necessary for a good fit. Assemble the drawer, without glue, and check for square. Disassemble and clean off any surface marks.

23 Apply glue and assemble the drawer. Cramp it together, check that it is square, and leave it to dry.

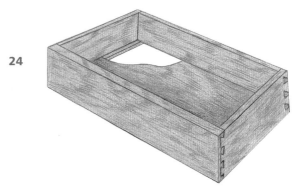

24

24 Measure the required size for the drawer bottom. The grain should run from side to side. Trim it to fit the groove at the front and sides (it passes underneath the back). The bottom is not glued, but is held in place by screwing or pinning where it passes under the drawer back.

25 When the drawer is dry, clean off in the joint areas. Try it in the drawer opening. Adjust for a good sliding fit.

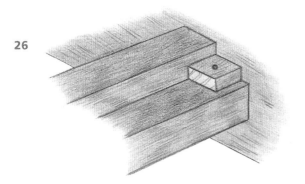

26 Fit the drawer stops as shown – it is easier to do this before fitting the top.

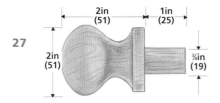

27 Make or buy a knob for the drawer. Drill a tight hole for the shaft and glue it into place. Secure with a wedge.

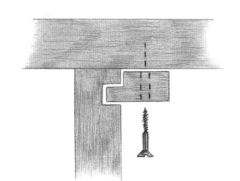

28 You can now fit the top. Using "buttons" is the usual method of doing this. These screw to the top, but are held in grooves in the side rails and are free to slide in order to allow for any movement of the wood. The step of the button should be slightly less than the distance between the groove and the rail edge in order to keep the top pulled downward. Make sure the screws are not too long. Fit two buttons at each end and two along each side.

29 Before fitting the top, plane the top surface to a good finish. Plane its edges smooth and bevel over the top edges and corners. Then fit as described in step 28.

30 The frame may be stained darker or given a finish appropriate for its use (see pages 108–13). The pine top may also be given a clear finish, but if it is for the kitchen it should be left untreated and kept clean by scrubbing.

Wall-Hung Cupboard

ABILITY LEVEL
Experienced

SIZE
27 x 20 x 9in (686 x 508 x 229mm)

MATERIALS
Pine

CUTTING LIST
CARCASS
2 sides
26 x 7 x ¾in (660 x 178 x 19mm)
1 top
18¼ x 7 x ¾in (457 x 178 x 19mm)
1 bottom
18¼ x 7 x ¾in (457 x 178 x 19mm)
1 mid shelf
18¼ x 6¾ x ¾in (457 x 171 x 19mm)
1 back
26 x 19 x ⅜in (660 x 483 x 10mm)

FACE FRAME (FRONT)
2 stiles
26 x 3 x ¾in (660 x 76 x 19mm)
2 rails
16 x 3 x ¾in (406 x 76 x 19mm)
1 mid rail
16 x 3 x ¾in (406 x 76 x 19mm)

DOOR
2 stiles
15 x 3 x ¾in (381 x 76 x 19mm)
2 rails
10 x 3 x ¾in (254 x 76 x 19mm)
1 panel
10 x 8 x ½in (254 x 203 x 12mm)

DRAWER
1 front
13 x 3 x ½in (330 x 76 x 12mm)
2 sides
7 x 3 x ½in (178 x 76 x 12mm)
1 back
13 x 2½ x ½in (330 x 64 x 12mm)
1 onset front
13½ x 3½ x ½in (343 x 89 x 12mm)
1 bottom
12 x 7 x ¼in (305 x 178 x 6mm)
4 guides
7 x ½ x ½in (178 x 12 x 12mm)
2 supports
7 x 5½ x ½in (178 x 140 x 12mm)

CORNICE
1 top rail
21 x 3 x ¾in (533 x 76 x 19mm)
2 side rails
9 x 3 x ¾in (229 x 76 x 19mm)

MOULDING
approx 9ft of ¾ x ¾in (2743 x 19 x 19mm)

Wall-mounted cupboards such as this could once be found in any room of the house: in the kitchen, for cooking utensils or for tinned or packaged foodstuffs and spices; in the bathroom – a cupboard much like this still makes an ideal medical cabinet; or in a sitting or family room, for housing books and important family papers. If needs be, a lock could easily be fitted, especially if medicines were to be kept inside. Cupboards used for storing food are often found with pierced fronts to allow fresh air to circulate inside to keep food fresh but the flies out. The wall-hung cupboard described in the project that follows, although rather elaborate for a country piece, is based on one said to have been made in Pennsylvania in about 1750.

Method

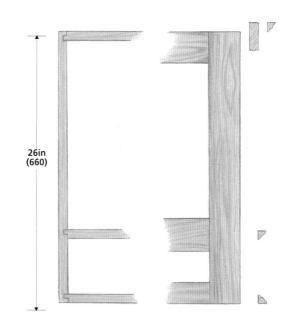

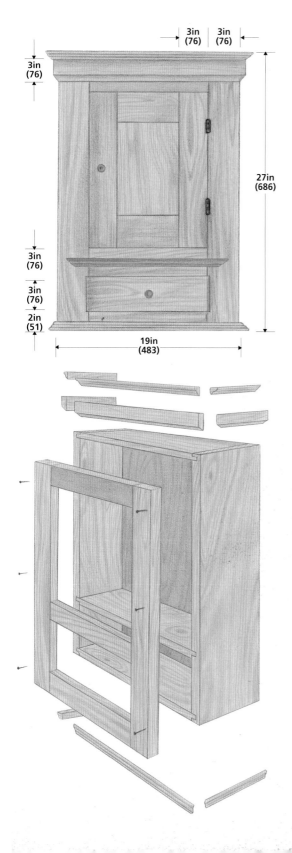

1 Select materials and cut all parts to size. Take care to cut all ends squarely and accurately (see page 94 for advice). Keep all related parts together – for example, drawer parts, carcass parts, etc.

2 Begin by planing and edge gluing the pieces needed to make wider boards, if necessary.

3

⅜in
(10)

⅜in
(10)

19in
(483)

26in
(660)

⅜in
(10)

7in
(178)

7in
(178)

¾in
(19)

3 Construct the carcass first. Mark out and cut the through housings, ¼in (6mm) deep, in the side pieces to accommodate the top, middle, and bottom shelves. Cut a ⅜in (10mm) rebate for the back (see page 101 for advice on rebates).

4 Test fit, without using glue, to check that everything fits and is square. Disassemble and clean off any surface marks.

5 Apply glue and assemble the carcass. Again, check that it is square and hold it together with cramps until it is dry.

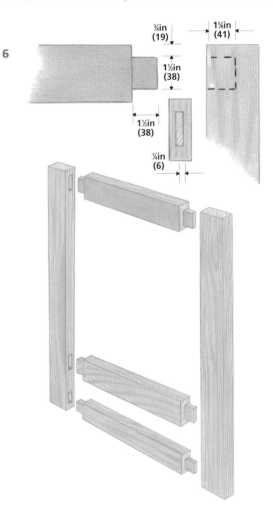

¾in
(19)

1⅝in
(41)

1½in
(38)

1½in
(38)

¼in
(6)

6

6 Make up the front face frame using mortises and tenons (see pages 104–6 for advice on making these joints). Check the lengths of the components. The frame can be slightly larger than the carcass to allow for planing to a flush fit later.

7 Mark out and cut the mortises into each of the stiles, and mark and cut the tenons on each end of the rails. Since the stiles and rails are ¾in (19mm) thick, the mortises and tenons will be ¼in (6mm).

8 Check that each joint is a good fit. Then test fit, without glue, and check that the frame is square. Disassemble and clean off any surface marks.

9 Apply glue and make up the front face frame. Hold it with cramps and check that it has not twisted out of square.

10 The door is of frame-and-panel construction and has haunched mortise and tenon joints. This, too, should be slightly oversized so that it can be planed to a good fit within the door-opening.

11 Cut a ¼in (6mm) wide, ¼in (6mm) deep groove along the inside edge of all four door frame pieces (see page 101) to accommodate the panel.

12 Mark out and cut the mortises into both stiles.

13 Mark out and cut the haunched tenons on each end of the rails. The haunch is trimmed to fit and fill the exposed ends of the grooves made in the stiles.

14 Test fit each joint and then assemble the door frame, without using glue, to check that it is square.

15 While the door frame is assembled, measure the opening for the door panel. Add ⅜in (10mm) to both the length and the width (to fit into the frame groove). Now disassemble the frame.

16 Cut the door panel to the precise dimensions determined in step 15. Plane a long bevel all around the panel, as shown in diagram 10, and test fit it in the door frame groove.

17

17 Assemble the door frame and panel, without using glue, bevel facing outward. Check for square and then disassemble and clean off any surface marks.

18 Glue and assemble the door, but do not glue in the panel. Hold the frame together with cramps and check for square.

19 Attach the front face frame to the carcass by gluing and nailing. Punch the nail heads below the surface and fill the indentations. Plane off the frame overlap.

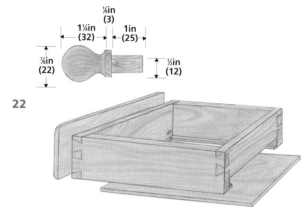

22

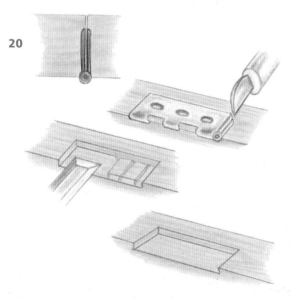

20

20 Try the door for size in the opening and then trim it to a tight fit. Mark the position of the hinges and chisel out the hinge housings. Test fit and hang the door.

21 To simplify the making of the drawer, through dovetail joints have been used (see pages 102–3 for advice). The onset, or lipped false front, conceals the joints at the front and also eliminates the need for any drawer stops.

22 Begin by making the drawer front fit the opening. Cut the back to the same length as the front, and the side pieces the same width as the front. Check that the ends are square and mark adjoining parts.

23 Now mark out and cut the dovetail "tails" on the drawer side pieces (see pages 102–3 for advice).

24 Mark out the dovetail "sockets" using the "tails" cut in step 23 as a template.

25 Cut the dovetail "sockets" (see page 103 for advice) and test fit each joint, but avoid handling them too often.

26 Assemble the drawer parts, without using glue, and check for square. Disassemble the drawer and clean off any surface marks ready for the next stage.

27 Apply glue and assemble the drawer. Cramp it together and check again for square. When dry, clean off surplus glue in the joint areas.

28 Fit the drawer bottom, with the grain running from side to side, on strips of wood glued and pinned on at the sides and front. Pin it, without glue, where it passes under the back piece.

29 Glue and nail the onset false front into position, with an equal overhang all around. Punch the nail holes below the surface and fill the indentations with woodfiller or a mixture of glue and sawdust. When the glue is thoroughly dry, round over the overhanging front edges.

30

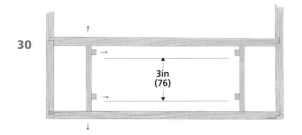

3in
(76)

30 The drawer runs between supports and simple guides, fitted as shown.

31 Cut the cornice pieces to length and mitre their mating ends. On the lower edges of each piece, plane a ½in (12mm) bevel.

32

32 Test fit and then glue and nail the cornice into place.

33 Mitre and test fit the top and bottom mouldings. Glue and pin them into position when you are satisfied. Apply the centre moulding.

34 Cut the back to size and pin it into its rebate.

35 Make or buy matching knobs for the door and drawer. Drill tight holes for these and glue them into place.

36 The finish on the original cupboard is matt blue paint applied over layers of earlier paint. See pages 110 and 113 for ways of achieving a similar antique paint finish.

Folk Bed

ABILITY LEVEL
Experienced

SIZE
80 x 56 x 44in (2032 x 1422 x 1118mm)

MATERIALS
Pine

CUTTING LIST
2 corner posts
44 x 3 x 3in (1118 x 76 x 76mm)
2 corner posts
34 x 3 x 3in (864 x 76 x 76mm)
1 headboard
53 x 32 x ¾in (1346 x 813 x 19mm)
1 footboard
53 x 22 x ¾in (1346 x 559 x 19mm)
2 side rails
77 x 6 x 1½in (1955 x 152 x 38mm)
2 slat rails
75 x 2 x 1in (1905 x 51 x 25mm)
12 slats
52 x 3 x 1in (1320 x 76 x 25mm)
4 wooden balls
3in (76mm) dia
4 bolts
6in (152mm)

These dimensions are designed for a 75 x 54in (1905 x 1372mm) mattress. However, it is best to measure the mattress to be used before starting this project and adjust dimensions as necessary.

See template pattern on page 121 for heart motif.

All measurements are given in inches, with the equivalents in millimetres indicated in brackets.

NOTE
After cleaning off all surface marks, you can apply a clear polish, stain, or paint (see pages 108–13 for different finishes).

The basic design for most beds stems from the the simple bedstock, known in the 18th century as the stump bedstead, with the legs of its wooden framework extended at one end and filled in with a plain headboard. The supporting wooden laths, which replaced a webbed base, gave way to the use of spring metal and, by the middle of the 19th century, the iron and brass bedstead had become fashionable. However, country makers continued to make wooden bedsteads and today they remain as popular as ever. This solid, substantial bed, with head- and footboards, has a distinctly folk art feel to it. The two heart-shaped cut-outs are a typical motif of the Tirol region in the Swiss Alps.

Method

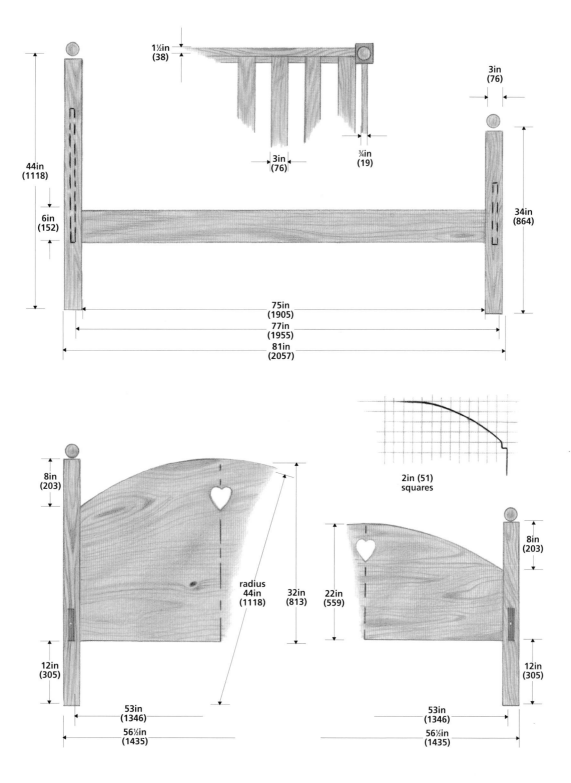

1½in
(38)

3in
(76)

3in
(76)

¾in
(19)

44in
(1118)

6in
(152)

34in
(864)

75in
(1905)

77in
(1955)

81in
(2057)

8in
(203)

radius
44in
(1118)

32in
(813)

12in
(305)

53in
(1346)

56½in
(1435)

2in (51)
squares

22in
(559)

8in
(203)

12in
(305)

53in
(1346)

56½in
(1435)

1 Begin by making up the head- and footboards by edge-joining narrower pieces of wood (see pages 100–101 for advice). Individual pieces should be as wide as possible so that there are not too many joints.

2 When gluing is complete and the work has dried, clean up the boards and check that they are flat. Cut them to the exact length and check that the ends are square.

3 Using the grid on the previous page mark out and cut the curved top edges of each board.

4 Mark out and cut the heart motifs. Use the template pattern on page 121. Round over all cut edges.

5 Cut the corner posts to length and plane or sand the surfaces smooth. The ball finials are optional and may be fitted later. Make pencil marks on one end of the posts, as shown below, to avoid confusion later when marking out for jointing.

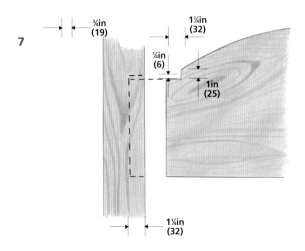

7 Each end board is notched at the top to fit the mortise and should be cut slightly short (see diagram). This is an allowance for any movement that may take place in the boards.

8 Test fit the end boards individually, without using glue, in their respective slots. Adjust if necessary by trimming the ends of the boards until the joints are tight and enter to their full depth. Disassemble and put the boards aside until later.

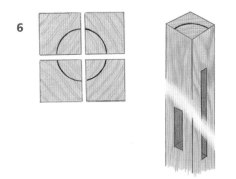

6 Head- and footboards are housed, at their full thickness, in mortises cut into the corner posts. Take measurements from the boards you have; these may differ from those given. Make the mortises a little undersized and trim the ends of the boards to a tight fit.

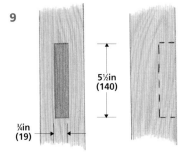

9 Mark out the correct adjacent face of each corner post for the mortises to accommodate the side rails. The pencil marks made on the end of the posts will help here. Cut these mortises (see pages 104–6 for advice).

10 Cut the side rails to length and make sure that the ends are square. Plane or sand the rails smooth.

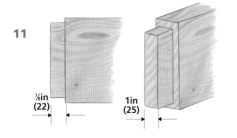

11

⅞in (22)   1in (25)

11 Mark out and cut the tenons on each end of the side rails (see pages 104–6 for advice).

12 Test fit the side rail tenons and the corner post mortises, without using glue. Adjust as necessary for a good fit.

13 The head- and footboards are permanently glued into their corner post joints. The side rail tenons are not glued but held in their corner post mortises by bed bolts, as shown, to allow easy assembly and a useful knock-down facility. Bolts can be bought or made using threaded studding.

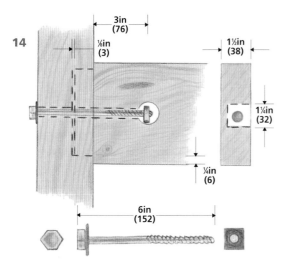

14

3in (76)   ⅛in (3)   1½in (38)   1¼in (32)   ¼in (6)   6in (152)

14 The diagrams show how to fit the bed bolts, but measurements may need to be altered to suit the bolts actually used. The nut recess is bored on the inside of the side rail. Place the post on its side on a bench, with the rail tenon in place in its mortise, and bore the through hole carefully with a carpenter's twist bit.

15 Try each joint by fitting the bolt and nut and tightening until the shoulders of the rail tenon come up tight against the corner post. Make identification marks on the rails and posts to aid reassembly. Disassemble.

16 If ball finials are to be fitted, find the centre of the corner posts and bore a hole to house the fixing dowel. Glue in place. Chamfer the long edges of each corner post and, if finials are not fitted, round over the top edges.

17 Now join the end boards to their respective corner posts. Place glue in the slot mortises, fit the end boards correctly and pull them in tight with cramps. Clean off any surplus glue. Leave to dry.

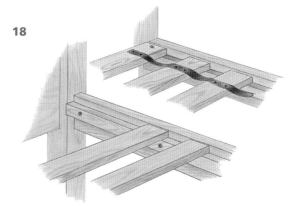

18

18 The mattress rests on slats, which are supported on rails glued and screwed to the inside of the side rails. Fix these rails so that the slats will be flush with, or slightly below, the top edge of the side rails.

19 Now assemble the bed frame. Make sure that the side rails fit correctly and that the bed bolts tighten fully. Cut the slats to fit across the bed frame. Space them out evenly. Slats may be loosely strung together, nailed or stapled, to two lengths of woven tape. Screw the top and bottom slats down and the assembly will stay in place.

What You Need to Know

Tools & Techniques

Most of the projects featured in this book require only the simplest of woodworking tools, so there is no need to have or buy an expensive or complicated kit. However, some basic knowledge of how to use these tools is assumed.

If you are a beginner, start with the projects which that been designed for the "novice" level and, by working through these, hopefully you will soon pick up the expertise required to undertake the more complicated "intermediate" and "experienced" projects that appear later in the book.

All of the projects have been designed to be completed using hand tools only. However, although immensely satisfying, working entirely with hand tools (as opposed to power tools) can be both tiring and time-consuming, as well as often requiring a high degree of skill. So, if you have power tools available – and you know how to use them safely and competently – there is no reason why you should not press them into service. In my own work I often use a combination of methods: power tools for the initial, often repetitive, work such as sawing to size and planing to thickness; a combination of power and hand tools for shaping and jointing; and hand tools for finishing and detailing.

The original country woodworker would have had few tools at his disposal, and these would have most probably been general-purpose implements, rather than specialist ones, used for all manner of jobs around the cottage or farm. An axe and an adze would have been used for chopping and riving, for example; a saw and a few chisels for cutting; a drawknife, spokeshave, rasp, and files for shaping; a plane for smoothing; a brace and bit for drilling holes; a hammer and nails for fastening; and a knife for cutting and trimming.

Construction methods, too, would have been all-purpose and relatively simple, using whatever timber was available and most suitable for the job in hand. The fundamental techniques of woodworking – shaping and jointing – have been known for thousands of years, and working methods evolved from applications such as house and barn construction, fence building, wheelwrighting, and so on. The joints used were basic to all forms of woodworking: the mortise and tenon of the shipwright and barn framer is larger and perhaps cruder than that of the furniture maker, but it is the same joint; the foot-long trenels (tree nails) of the trestle builder are no different in principle to the smaller pegs used to secure the joints of a country-made chair.

The techniques employed in the projects section of this book would have been used as a matter of course by the early country woodworker, and while the methods of certain types of construction may not have been part of the daily routine, he would certainly have been familiar with them. However, the exact way and sequence in which the steps are carried out would no doubt have varied according to an individual woodworker's knowledge and level of skill. In the projects described, all of the methods given follow traditional principles that are accepted and in use today, but they are open to individual interpretation.

BASIC TOOLS

It is not easy to say what a basic set of tools is for a modern woodworker – much depends on what is to be made, on personal preferences, and what is affordable. But whatever you decide on, always buy the best quality you can afford, and then take good care of the tools that you have. Working with poorly made or misused tools is a handicap nobody needs.

The list on page 90 includes those tools required for the projects and it concentrates mainly on hand tools, together with a few of the most helpful and time-saving power tools.

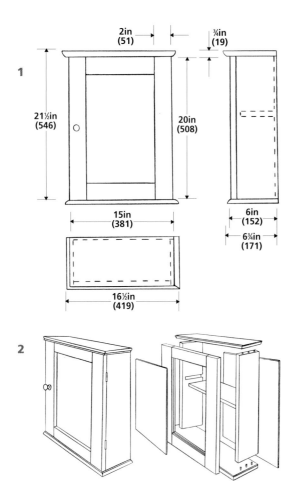

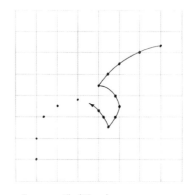

Squares = ½in (12mm)

DRAWINGS AND PATTERNS

Before undertaking any project in wood, it is helpful to have a drawing or plan showing the general shape and main dimensions of the piece, together, preferably, with more detailed drawings of specific parts. There are two main ways in which drawings such as these may be presented.

The first is known as an orthographic presentation, which normally shows three views – front and end views, plus a top, or plan, view. **(1)**

The second form of presentation is a perspective drawing, which may also be in the form of an "exploded" view. **(2)**

Sometimes it is helpful to show detailed parts of a project, such as curves, as a pattern or template. Where these cannot be shown full size, they are drawn on a scale grid. Each small square of the grid represents ½in (12mm), 1in (25mm), or 2in (51mm), as indicated, and from this you can lay out a full-sized pattern using grid squares of the correct size. **(3)**

WORKBENCH AND VICE

On the practical side, a space in which to work and a sturdy table or bench are your first requirements. This bench or table should also have some reliable method of holding wood securely while you are working on it. This usually means fitting a vice of some type, but you can also use other devices, such as bench stops or dogs and G cramps of various sizes (see page 97).

A cast-iron carpenter's vice with wooden jaw facings is ideal. However, if you have an engineer's vice, you will need to cover its iron jaws to prevent them biting into and damaging the wood. For light work, you can temporarily clamp a vice to the edge of your bench.

A useful device is a bench-hook, which you can easily make up yourself **(4)**. It can be gripped in a vice or held against the edge of your bench to provide a useful holding stop for work being chiselled or sawn, as well as helping to prevent damage to the bench top during these operations.

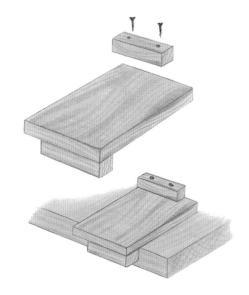

4

6

7

MEASURING AND MARKING OUT

Before you start making up any piece, you need to check that the wood is the right size and that it is straight and square and not warped. If you buy wood "ready planed" or "prepared" it should be fine to work with, but its machine-planed surface will require hand planing or sanding. Identify the best wide surface and an edge, plane them square if necessary, and then mark them with face-side and face-edge marks – see top of diagram **5** for the conventional method. From then on, all marking out and gauging should be done on, or from, these surfaces.

When you need to cut a board to length, make certain to check that the starting end is sound (not damaged or split) as well as square. If necessary, mark off a "waste" piece from the suspect end (single line in diagram **5**), measuring the length of the board from that mark. For a small board you can use a ruler, but a retractable steel tape is quicker when measuring a long board.

5

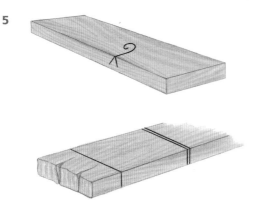

When drawing the line to indicate the length of board you want, mark it accurately and squarely by using a try square or an all-metal combination square. For precise work, make an allowance for the width of the saw cut, or kerf (double lines in diagram **5**). Always saw on the waste side of the line, and if you want to cut several pieces from the same board, allow a generous ⅛in (3mm) waste strip for the kerf between each piece.

A well-sharpened HB-grade pencil is suitable for most of the marking out you will encounter. But for really accurate results the point of a sharp knife has many advantages, especially when marking wood across the grain. The knife point severs the surface fibres of the wood and leaves a clean edge after cutting. A traditional carpenter's marking knife has a thick, bevelled skew blade for this purpose – usually ground for right-hand users only. A small, lock-blade pocket knife is also recommended.

To mark lines parallel to an edge, you should be using a marking gauge, which is mainly used to gauge wood to both width and thickness prior to hand planing. Adjust it to give the mark you need by setting the required distance between the movable head and the pointed spur. To mark a line, press the head firmly against the edge of the work and push or pull the gauge away from you. Use a light stroke to reduce the danger of the point digging in and following the grain. **(6)**

For less precise work, hold a pencil and your fingers as shown – this "trick of the trade" is known as finger gauging. **(7)**

There are two other types of gauge you should be familiar with: the cutting gauge and the mortise gauge. The cutting gauge has a small blade instead of the marking gauge's spur, and it is most effective when marking across the grain. The mortise gauge, as its name suggests, is mainly used for marking out mortise and tenon joints. It has two pointed spurs – the inner one is adjustable so that you can mark out parallel lines of different distances from each other.

Compasses and dividers are most often used to mark circles or arcs, and you can use dividers to transfer measurements and to "step-off" equal divisions along a line.

SAWS AND SAWING
There are several different types of hand saw, some designed for general use and others for more specialized applications. The shape and size of the saw blade, and the number and configuration of its teeth, are what distinguish one type from another.

8

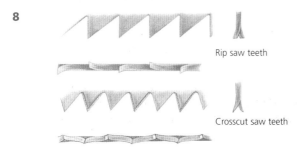

Rip saw teeth

Crosscut saw teeth

Rip saws, for example, are large, have between 4 and 6 teeth every 1in (25mm), and are used for cutting (ripping) with the grain. The shorter crosscut saw has between 7 and 12 teeth every 1in (25mm). Both types are used mainly in the initial preparation of timber and for cutting boards to size. **(8)**

The tenon saw is the best-known example of what are called back saws. These saws have thin blades stiffened and weighted by a folded metal strip, usually brass, along their back edges, and they are used for accurate bench work and for cutting joints. Back saws are available in different sizes and can have from 12 to more than 20 teeth every 1in (25mm). The smallest type of

back saw with the greatest number of teeth and finest cut is generally known as a dovetail saw. Saws for cutting curved shapes use a narrow, flexible blade that easily breaks. In some saws, this problem is overcome by holding the blade under tension in a frame. The earliest type, known as a bow saw, has a blade held in a wooden frame tensioned by means of a twisted cord. More modern designs rely on a spring-steel frame and one of these, the coping saw, uses disposable blades that fit into pins tensioned by twisting the handle of the saw. You can fit the blade so that it cuts either on the pull stroke or on the push stroke. To make an internal cut through a piece of wood, first drill a small hole through the work, pass the blade through, and then fit it into the saw frame. The coping saw is used to remove waste wood from a dovetail joint (see page 103).

If you always make sure your saw is sharp, then sawing by hand should not be too difficult. Never force the saw into the wood. This is hard work and it tends to cause the blade to twist and jam in the kerf. For trouble-free sawing, support or hold your work securely, work with firm, even, fluid strokes, and use the whole length of the blade to cut with. Begin carefully – with a tenon saw pull back on the first strokes to establish a start – and work to the waste side of the line.

All of these sawing operations can be carried out with power tools, either portable or fixed. You can use a circular saw for straight cuts, while for straight and curved cuts you have a choice of the versatile jigsaw, saber saw, a machine fret saw, or a band saw.

PLANES AND PLANING
The type of plane generally known as a bench plane is used to reduce the thickness or width of a piece of wood to the size required and to straighten or smooth a surface. Other types of specialist plane are used for grooving, moulding, and shaping; some of these may be multi-purpose planes.

There are various types and sizes of bench plane, but they are all constructed in much the same way. Early planes had wooden bodies, or stocks, fitted with a blade, or cutting iron, held in place with a wooden wedge. The all-metal plane appeared in the middle of the 19th century and, due to the fact that it could be more easily and precisely adjusted, it became the preferred tool – although wooden planes are still in use today.

The metal jack plane is a "jack-of-all-trades". Its main use is to bring timber down to size, but, if it is fitted with a suitably ground and sharpened blade (see page 98), you can also use it for general straightening and smoothing. The length of a jack plane varies between 14 and 18in (355 and 457mm), making it particularly useful for planing long edges for jointing purposes. The metal smoothing plane **(9)** is made in the same way as the jack plane, but it is shorter in length – 8 to 10in (203 to 254mm). It, too, can be used as a general-purpose plane, but it is intended mainly for finishing a surface after a jack plane or a machine plane has been used. Light planing with a sharp and fine-set smoothing plane can produce an excellent surface finish.

When planing a piece of work, make sure that the wood is securely and safely held in place. When edge planing, grip the work in a bench vice; for surface planing, either cramp the wood to the bench top or hold it between pairs of bench dogs. In order to achieve a smooth finish you have to plane with the grain of the wood, and not against it. On the end grain, plane halfway from each side to avoid splitting out the far edge. The lower cutting angle of the smaller block plane is best for end grain work. As a general rule, when any plane is not in use, place it on its side on the bench in order to prevent damage to the blade.

For a particularly fine finish, especially on hardwoods, a cabinet scraper is the ideal tool. This device consists simply of a thin piece of good-quality steel, the edge of which is especially shaped and sharpened to remove a delicate shaving of wood – like a butterfly's wing – when held and

flexed between the fingers and thumbs of both hands and pushed forward over the wood at a suitable angle.

Although not really a plane, a spokeshave cuts in a similar way. Older, wooden-stocked versions have forged, tanged blades, which may be more difficult to adjust than a modern spokeshave but produce an excellent finish.

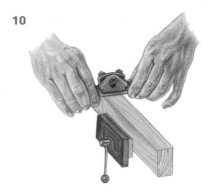

Modern, metal spokeshaves are available in either flat or half-round versions. Used with a pushing action, a spokeshave makes chamfers and smooths narrow curved edges **(10)**. A drawknife, which is used mainly for roughing-out work and for rounding and shaping, is drawn toward you with a firm pulling action. Drawknives are best suited to working on green (unseasoned) wood.

The specialist planes used for such tasks as grooving have become more or less obsolete due to the portable electric router, which does the same work with greater speed. However, many of these hand planes are still available and can be used.

Electric planers can be either portable or fixed. Hand-held electrical planers are not recommended, and fixed machines can be expensive. Wherever possible, it is best to buy-in wood that is "ready planed" or "prepared" to size. If wood is machine planed it will need to be finished off with a hand plane, or sanded, in order to remove the rippled surface left by the rotary cutting action produced by all power planers.

CHISELS AND GOUGES

Chisels for woodworking are of several different types and come in many different sizes, depending on the work they are to perform; firmer, bevel-edged, paring, and mortise are just some of the names given to them. "Chisels" with a curved cutting edge should more correctly be called "gouges". In addition, there are chisels and gouges made specifically for lathe work and for wood carving. Chisels are categorized by size – for example, the width of the cutting edge – and gouges by size and "sweep" – the degree of curvature of the cutting edge.

11

For general woodworking the bevel-edge chisel has some clear advantages over the others, since its shape makes it particularly suitable for reaching into tight corners, cleaning out joints, and so on. You can, if necessary, strike the top of its handle lightly with a wooden mallet to get extra force behind its cutting action. Keep your chisels sharp at all times – it is easier to have an accident when forcing a blunt chisel to cut than when guiding a sharp chisel into the wood. And never hold your piece of work with one hand while using a chisel with the other – secure the wood in place and keep both hands behind the chisel's cutting edge. Make your first cuts across the grain of the wood to sever the fibres and try to cut with the grain at all other times. **(11)**

SHAPING AND SMOOTHING

Although a cutting tool produces a better surface finish and is satisfying to use, there are times when you need to use other implements for shaping and smoothing. Rasps and files are abrading tools made from hardened steel. Rasps have coarse, triangular-shaped teeth and, because they remove wood quite quickly, they are used for rough shaping. Files, which come in a variety of "cuts" from

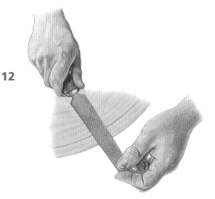

12

coarse to fine, are used more for smoothing. All can be readily bought in flat and half-round shapes – some files in round (or "rat's tail") section. **(12)**

Modern abrading tools usually have tungsten-carbide grit welded to both rigid and flexible substrates, while another design incorporates a disposable blade of thin, hardened steel perforated with many sharp-edged holes. These holes form multiple cutting edges, but they leave a rough surface that requires smoothing.

For many shaping operations you can use electric belt, disc, and drum sanders, while orbital sanders are often recommended for surface finishing. These devices can save you a lot of time, especially in production work, but they do not always leave a satisfactory finish. They also produce a lot of fine dust. Either the tool should have its own dust bag or you will need to wear a dust-protection mask or respirator.

DRILLS AND DRILLING

Traditionally, wood-boring bits or auger bits fixed into a brace of wood and metal were used for drilling holes in wood. These were replaced by all-metal braces using interchangeable bits, or drills, together with another form of hand drill known as the wheelbrace. Metal braces, some with a ratchet action, and wheelbraces are still in use today, but the portable electric hand drill is the most popular and commonly used device when drilling holes in wood. You can buy a vertical stand to convert an ordinary electric hand drill into a simple but effective bench drill, while the multispeed drilling machine, available in both bench and floor-standing models, is more suited to heavy and repetitive types of work.

Whatever type of drill you decide to use, there is a wide range of drill bits from which to choose. For general drilling, up to about ½in (12mm) diameter, ordinary twist bits, or engineer's drills, are suitable (**13**A). An improvement on this design is the modified twist bit known as the dowel bit, or brad point bit (**13**B). For more accurate drilling and for large-diameter holes, the saw-tooth Forstner bit is recommended (**13**C), but this type of drill bit requires a power drill. If you are using a brace, the old type of centre bits (**13**D) and auger bits (**13**E) are probably best. For countersinking after drilling, use a rose-head countersink (**13**F).

13

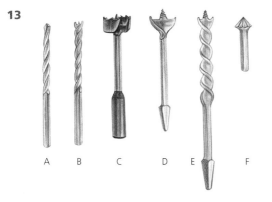

A   B   C   D   E   F

HAMMERS, SCREWDRIVERS, AND RELATED TOOLS

For the projects described in this book, a medium-weight cross pein hammer is most generally suitable. Hold small nails and panel pins between your fingers and start off using the tapered pein before switching to the face of the hammer to drive them home. A pair of pincers is useful for removing nails that bend or break. A wooden mallet is used mainly when you are working with a chisel or gouge, but you may also find it useful at the assembly stage of some jobs. Choose a medium-sized mallet with a head made from seasoned beech.

Screwdrivers are available in a wide range of sizes and types, with handles in different shapes and made from a variety of materials. What matters most is the size and shape of the end, or tip, in relation to the size and type of screw you are using. The oldest, and perhaps the most common type of screwdriver is the flat-tip blade made to fit the traditional slotted screw heads; more modern types include various patterns of cross-head screws and screwdrivers. A flat-tip blade should fit snugly into the screw slot. Make sure that it is neither too large nor too small or you may damage the screw.

For starting screws, and sometimes nails, in softwood you may find a bradawl useful. A bradawl makes a guide hole and reduces the danger of the wood splitting. Start a screwdriver-tipped bradawl across the grain of the wood. When nailing or screwing into hardwood, and sometimes into softwood, it is best to drill clearance and pilot holes (see page 100). You can use a pin punch or nail set to sink nail heads below the surface of your work.

CRAMPS

You will find that cramps are useful items for holding work securely in place temporarily, or for applying pressure to pieces of wood while glue dries and bonds them together.

14

The most common kind of cramp is the G cramp **(14)**, and there are several types and sizes from which to choose. The size is usually quoted as the maximum distance between the jaws of the cramp, and this may range from 2in (51mm) to 12in (305mm). For holding larger or wider pieces of work, usually during the assembly stages, you should use sash or bar cramps. These consist of a steel bar drilled through at intervals to hold a pin that retains a sliding jaw or shoe. At the opposite end there is an adjustable jaw that takes up the final pressure. Always use cramps with protective blocks of wood to prevent the surface of your work from becoming damaged. There are numerous modern variations of both these standard types of cramps, some better than others.

ABRASIVES AND ADHESIVES

The words "sandpaper" and "sanding" are still frequently used as general terms for abrasive sheet materials and their use. However, sand is no longer to be found on abrasive sheets. Instead, materials such as powdered glass, crushed garnet, aluminum oxide, or silica carbide are used. These are deposited as grits on to various backings – cloth or paper – and in different densities and grit sizes. Sheets are normally classified by the type and grade of abrasive and by a number system related to grit size – the higher the number, the finer the abrasive. For hand sanding, many people prefer the pink-coloured garnet paper in grades 100, 150, and 220. Always sand with, not across, the grain of the wood, and wrap the paper around a sanding block to help keep the surface of the wood flat. Even if you use a power sander, you will still probably have to finish off by hand sanding.

The term "gluing-up" may in fact mean using any one of numerous adhesives that are now available. Traditionally, animal glue was used – it was all there was – and this had to be melted and applied hot. Today, there are upward of a dozen different types of adhesive, some intended for specialist applications. Those types based on PVA (polyvinyl acetate) are good, general-purpose glues, available for both indoor and outdoor use. Where a high level of water resistance is required, be sure to use a synthetic resin adhesive.

SHARPENING TOOLS

Sharp tools are a prerequisite for producing good-quality work – a dull cutting edge makes work difficult and is potentially dangerous. More cut hands result from pushing too hard with a blunt chisel than from working with one with a well-sharpened blade.

Sharpening takes in both grinding and honing. Grinding is carried out on a revolving grindstone, which usually leaves a coarse finish unsuitable as a cutting edge. After grinding, tools then have to be honed, or whetted, usually on a sharpening stone – either an oil-stone or a water-stone – to produce a sharp cutting edge. In normal use, tools can be honed several times before regrinding becomes necessary. Many grindstones are electrically driven and most have narrow abrasive wheels

revolving at about 3,000rpm (revolutions per minute) and are used dry. The danger here is that the steel being sharpened may overheat, and become soft as a result. The only way to avoid this happening is to dip the metal constantly in water to cool it. Machines with wider wheels revolving at only about 150–200rpm are more suitable.

Sharpening stones, usually oil-stones, come in three grades – coarse, medium, and fine – with the medium and fine grades being the most generally useful. Both natural and artificial stones are available. You should protect all types of oil-stone in a wooden box when they are not in use, and make sure that the surface is always lubricated with thin oil. The oil reduces the friction and floats off the fine metal residue produced by the sharpening process, which would otherwise clog the pores of the stone, causing the surface to glaze and become ineffective. Some stones use water as a lubricant. These stones are rather soft and easily damaged, but they do produce a fine edge. For really good results, the surface of your sharpening stone must be perfectly flat, so remember always to use the full width of the stone when sharpening tools.

14

When you buy new edge-cutting tools, such as planes and chisels, the blades supplied are ground but not honed. In order to hone a blade at the correct angle, hold it in both hands and place the ground bevel (which is about 25°) flat on the surface of the stone. Then raise your hands slightly to give an angle of about 30°. Using moderate pressure, rub the blade back and forth along the full length of the stone's surface. This produces a fine burr, or wire edge, on the back of the blade (you can easily feel it with your thumb). Turn the blade over and, keeping it absolutely flat on the stone, rub the burr away to produce a sharp cutting edge. **(14)** Check your results by holding the blade, edge up, to the light. Any bluntness will reflect light and show as a white line. For a superior cutting edge, strop the blade on a piece of leather dressed with oil and a mild abrasive.

One of the problems many beginners experience when honing, is rocking the tool or blade. This rounds the bevel over and stops it cutting properly. Maintaining the blade at the correct angle to the stone throughout the process can also cause problems. Gripping the blade firmly and keeping your wrists stiff help to combat the first problem, while a useful aid for both is the honing guide. This device runs on rollers and holds the blade firmly at precisely the correct honing angle to the stone while you push it back and forth.

WORKING METHODS
JOINING WOOD

There are numerous ways of joining pieces of wood together. Some involve metal fastenings, such as nails or screws, or use wooden dowels, while some rely entirely on the adhesion of glued surfaces or a combination of these methods. In others, the wooden components themselves are shaped into interlocking joints, such as mortise and tenons, dovetails, and so on, which form, when glued, permanent constructions.

These jointing techniques have evolved slowly over centuries and few of them can be improved on. However, in recent times, the increased use of man-made composite materials – plywood, chipboard, and MDF (medium-density fibreboard), for example – and the requirements of ease and speed of manufacture and assembly have resulted in the introduction of other methods of fastening and joining, such as the so-called knock-down fittings and other instant-jointing systems. However, in this book, the emphasis is on the use of solid, seasoned wood and the traditional methods of jointing, and only those techniques required to make the projects will be included.

Using nails Nails are available in a wide range of types and sizes. The selection illustrated here includes those required in the projects. Nails are made of a variety of materials, including steel, galvanized steel, brass, copper, and aluminium, and are known generally as wire nails or common nails, round and oval, and panel pins. Steel nails are suitable for most jobs – oval types reduce the risk of the wood splitting and you can punch them below the surface for a neat finish. For light work, and in some furniture making, panel pins are more suitable, and these too can be punched below the surface of your work to make a hidden fixing.

15

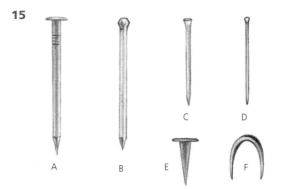

15 (A) Round wire nail, (B) Oval nail, (C) Lost-head nail, (D) Panel pin, (E) Tack or stud, (F) Staple.

Always use a nail or pin of suitable length. Long pins tend to bend easily, so support them between your forefinger and thumb and take care when knocking them in. Short pins may be difficult to hold, so try pushing them through a piece of stiff card held between your finger and thumb.

Pins used in conjunction with glue can make quite a strong joint. Strength is improved, especially on wide boards, if "dovetail nailing" is used. To make any nailed assembly easier, tap the nail or pin almost through the top piece first, apply the glue, and then position the pieces of wood together and knock the nail or pin all the way in. When working with hardwoods, which tend to split easily, it is best to predrill holes slightly smaller than the nails or pins to be used. For a neat finish, punch the nails or pins below the surface of the wood using a small nail punch or nail set and hammer. The punch should have a concave tip to prevent it slipping off the pin or nail head. Fill the holes left on the surface with a woodfiller or with a mixture of glue and sawdust.

Using screws Screws are used for joining pieces of wood together and for fitting hardware such as hinges, handles, and so on.

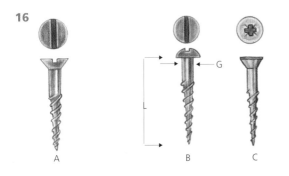

16

They are classified by length (**16**L); the thickness of the shank, or gauge (**16**G); and type of head. They are made in steel or brass and there are also several steel-coated varieties, such as chromium and zinc. The size is specified by length and the gauge by a number – the larger the number, the thicker the screw. Head types are basically either countersunk or flat head (**16**A), designed to go flush with or below the surface of the wood; or round head (**16**B), designed to sit on the surface. Screws may have the traditional straight slot for use with a conventional screwdriver, or be cross headed (**16**C) for use with an appropriate cross-head screwdriver.

For most work in the projects section, countersunk, slotted steel screws are used. However, with oak you must always use brass screws to prevent the tannin in the wood corroding the screws.

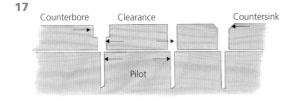

17
Counterbore   Clearance   Countersink

Pilot

Drilled holes are necessary when joining wood with screws, and when fitting hardware. With hardwoods, drill a clearance hole – one fractionally larger than the screw diameter – through the top piece, and a pilot hole – one smaller than the diameter of the screw threads – to the full length of the screw. In softwoods, the top clearance hole should be drilled, but you can use a bradawl for making the pilot hole. Use a countersink to recess the surface or counterbore the top and fill the surface with a wooden plug if you intend to conceal the head completely. Make sure you use the correct size of screwdriver for the size of screw, and press down firmly on the screw head as it is turned to prevent damage to the slot. Soft steel screws are easily damaged. **(17)**

Using adhesives Using an appropriate adhesive is often the most satisfactory way to join wood to wood, especially when it is used with one of the interlocking types of joint or when reinforced by nails or screws. For the glue to have maximum strength, you must first clean the parts that are to come into contact to remove any dust or loose wood that could create gaps – don't use glue as a space filler if you want a good joint. Then you must keep the pieces in tight contact until the glue is properly dry (see the manufacturer's recommendations), usually by cramping them together.

Plan the gluing-up stage of your work carefully. Have a clear, dust-free area in which to work and first of all test fit the pieces together (without using glue) to make sure that everything fits properly and is square. Have your glue and a damp cloth to hand; cramps should be ready and set to the right size with protective blocks available if needed. Use enough glue to prevent a dry joint but not so much that you create a messy clean-up job afterwards. Wipe away any surplus glue with a damp cloth. Bear in mind that glue marks can mar the appearance of some surface finishes.

MAKING JOINTS

Edge jointing When a wide piece of wood is called for, it may be necessary to join two narrower pieces together, edge to edge. The simplest and most satisfactory method is to use the plain rubbed joint. For this to work, you need to make sure that the mating edges are true and square along their entire length. You can avoid making the common error of planing more off the ends by planing the middle fractionally hollow. Planing the two edges at the same time helps accuracy. To test your results, hold the edges together and up to the light to identify any gaps.

18

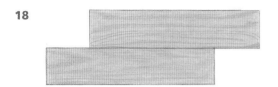

When you are satisfied, apply glue to one of the adjoining edges, press the edges together, and rub them backward and forward a few times. This removes any air from the joint and rubs the glue into the fibres – which gives the joint its name. **(18)**

19

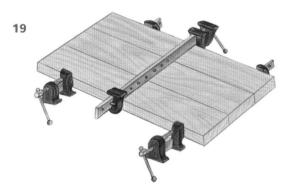

To hold the edges in tight contact, a minimum of three sash or bar cramps are needed, placed as shown. Tighten the middle one first. Check your work for flatness, clean off any surplus glue, and leave it to dry overnight. Plane or, preferably, scrape the joint area clean if necessary afterwards. **(19)**

The plain rubbed joint is fine for most work, but for larger surfaces, such as table tops, you can use a similar joint strengthened with dowels or by a loose tongue. To make a wider board, purchased tongue-and-groove boards can be glued together. **(20)**

20

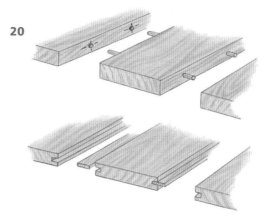

Grooves and rebates Although not strictly joints by themselves, grooves and rebates form parts of joints. A groove is a narrow channel cut usually along the length of a component, and a rebate is a recess along an edge, either with or across the grain. Both may be used to hold panels in place. Special-purpose all-metal planes are available for making grooves and rebates. A rebate plane will only cut a rebate, while a plough plane will tackle rebates and grooves. There are various multiplanes that will also do both, and other work besides. When using these planes, make short cuts beginning at the far end of the work and finish off with light continuous cuts.

The portable electric router, fitted with interchangeable cutters, has now taken over the work once performed by these different hand tools. When it is used with a suitable guide fence or with a manufactured or custom-built routing table, the portable router is safe, accurate, and quick.

Housing joint This type of joint comprises a narrow trench or wide groove cut across the grain of a piece of wood into which the end of another piece, such as a shelf, is fitted. Housings may be full thickness (of the shelf) or bare-faced, meaning that the shelf thickness is reduced to fit a narrower housing, and they can be either made through or stopped, as shown **(21)**. You can cut the joint entirely by hand, with a little help from a drilling machine if you like (see over the page), or you can use an electric router.

21

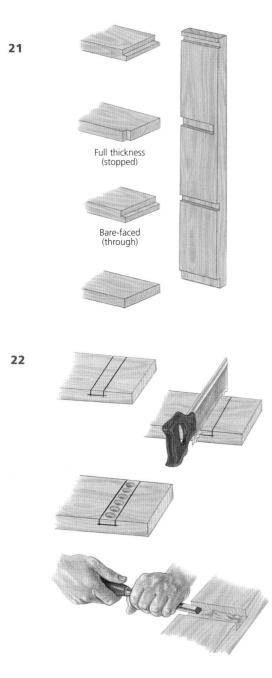

Full thickness
(stopped)

Bare-faced
(through)

22

with a sharp marking knife. Gauge the depth of the joint – which is usually ⅓ the thickness of the side piece – from the inside face. Securely cramp the work to the bench. Using a sharp ¾in (19mm) chisel, cut into the knifed lines on the waste side to form a guide groove for the saw. Saw down to the depth of the housing joint and then chisel out the waste wood, working in toward the centre from both ends where possible. You can use a drill to remove the bulk of the waste wood. Smooth the bottom of the joint and try the shelf for a fit. If necessary, plane a shaving off the underside of the shelf until you get a tight fit. **(22)**

Where one piece of wood meets another at a corner, as, for example, in a box-like construction, you can use similar housing joints. If the housing is full thickness it becomes, in effect, a cross-grain rebate, and you should secure it with glue and nails. However, a bare-faced housing is preferable in most circumstances and, if well made, this joint is strong enough using glue alone.

Dovetail joints You can obtain a much stronger corner joint using a dovetail joint, which is also particularly good for drawers. The strength of this joint lies in the increased gluing area and the interlocking shapes.

23

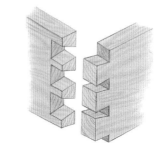

There are several types of dovetail, the simplest being the through dovetail **(23)**. In this, the end-grain portions of the joint, the tails and pins (the bits in between the tail sockets), are visible on both sides. In the lapped dovetail, often used on drawer fronts, the end grain is concealed on one face.

In drawer construction always cut the tails on the side pieces. Cut the materials to the required length and square across the end. Number, or otherwise identify, the

Begin by measuring the thickness of the shelf (or the bare-faced tongue made on the end of the shelf) and set out the position of the shelves on the supporting side pieces. Make the width of the housing joints fractionally less than the thickness of the shelves to ensure a tight fit. After checking, mark the cutting lines across the grain

matching ends. For through dovetails, where the front
and sides are the same thickness of wood, mark out and
cut the components as follows:

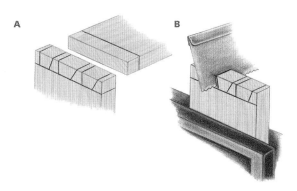

A Set a marking (or cutting) gauge to the thickness of
the wood and mark the ends of each piece all around –
this is the depth line of the joint. Mark out the tails first,
using either a T-bevel or a dovetail template. The tails
should be evenly spaced and the marked positions
squared across the end.

B With the wood held upright in a vice, carefully saw
on the waste side, using a dovetail or some other back
saw, down to the depth line as shown above.

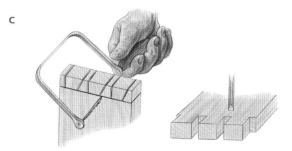

C Remove the bulk of the waste wood using a coping
saw and then finish removing the waste from both sides
with a sharp bevel-edge chisel.

D Mark out the sockets using the mating tails as a
template. Hold the component to be marked upright
in a vice and support the tail piece on it as shown. Align

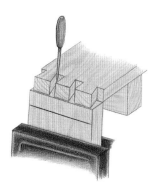

the tails carefully and mark clearly with a knife and square
lines down to the depth line.

E Cut away the waste wood as before, remembering to
cut on the waste side of the marked lines, and clean out
the joint with a sharp chisel. Test fit the joint and adjust
as necessary with a chisel.

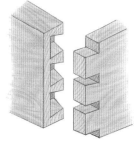

For lapped dovetails, the front piece is usually thicker than
the sides – this extra thickness forms the lap that conceals
the tails **(24)**. Prepare your materials as described for
through dovetails and, after deciding on the length of the
tails (which are often equal to the thickness of the sides
for convenience), set a marking gauge and mark the ends
of the side pieces all around. Mark the front piece along
the end and on the inside surfaces. Cut the tails and mark
out the sockets as described for the through dovetail.

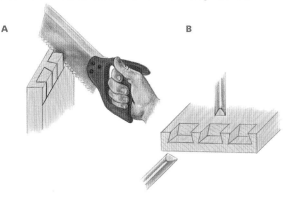

A With the front piece held upright in a vice, carefully saw at an angle down to the gauged lines on the inside surface and lap. Remember to cut on the waste side of the lines.

B With the piece secured flat on the bench, chisel out the waste wood beginning with vertical cuts (across the grain) and horizontal cuts. Use a sharp bevel-edge chisel and get right into the corners of the sockets. Test fit the joint and adjust as necessary.

You can cut dovetails by machine and these are usually recognizable by the even size and spacing of the pins and tails. However, modern jigs allow you to use a router to cut dovetails that are indistinguishable from hand-cut joints.

25

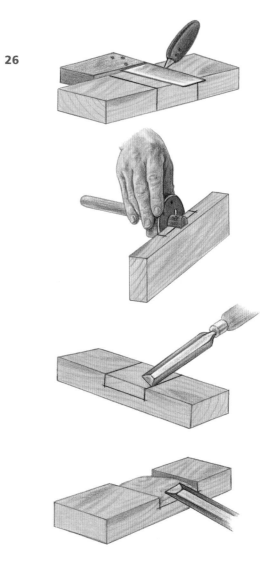

Cross-halving, or cross-lapped, joint Where two pieces of wood (usually of the same thickness) are to cross each other at right angles, and you want the surfaces to remain flush, you will have to use a cross-halving, or cross-lapped, joint. **(25)**

Plane the materials to size and square and mark the position of the joint full width and square across each piece using a sharp knife. Also mark the lines squared down the sides in pencil. Set a marking gauge to half the thickness of the wood and mark in the depth of the joint equally on both pieces. Chisel a sloping groove into the knifed lines (on the waste side) to make a guide for the saw, and then saw vertically down to the gauged line indicating the depth of the joint. Chisel out the waste wood, working from both sides in so that it is smooth and flat. **(26)**

Mortise and tenon joints The strongest as well as the most commonly used type of framing joint is the mortise and tenon. Although there are many variations of this joint, only three are considered here: the stub, or blind, mortise and tenon; the haunched mortise and tenon; and the more specialized double mortise and tenon. The main parts of each of these joints are the mortise, which is a recess or slot cut into (usually) the upright member or stile, and the tenon, which is a reduced projection on the end of the mating piece (generally called the rail), made to fit tightly into the mortise.

Plane the materials true and square, making sure that they are square across the ends. Where mortises come close to the end, it is usual practice to leave some extra length to the stiles initially to prevent the wood splitting. These projections are sawn off later.

A Cut the rails, remembering to allow for the length of both tenons. Mark the required length and square around with a sharp knife. This is the shoulder line of the tenon.

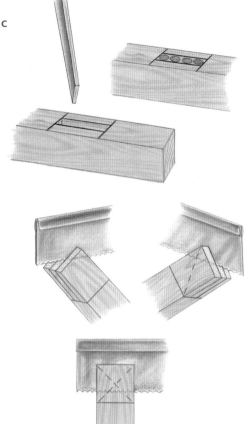

C

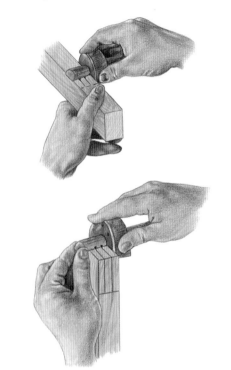

B

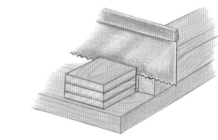

D

D Now cut the tenons. With the rail held in a vice, saw down both cheeks to the shoulder line, cutting on the waste side of the marked lines, with a tenon saw in three stages, as shown. Then, with the rail held to the bench, chisel a sloping groove into the knifed shoulder line, on the waste side, to make a guide for the saw.

B Mark out the positions of the mortises. The width required is the width of the tenons. Set the spurs of a mortise gauge to a chisel-width equal or close to a third the thickness of the rail. Use the gauge at this setting to mark the thickness of tenon all around and also to complete the marking of the mortise.

E

C Cut the mortises first. If you are doing this by hand, it helps to drill vertically down between the marked lines with a smaller-sized drill to remove the bulk of the waste wood, and then use a chisel to clean and square the joint. Make mortises ⅛in (3mm) deeper than the length of the tenon.

E Saw vertically down to the previously made saw cut to remove the cheek waste. Finally, mark the reduction in tenon width and saw off the waste.

F

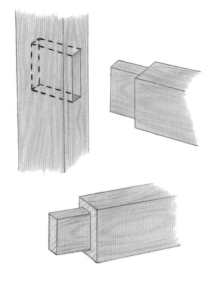

F Trim the tenon to a good fit in the mortise. Aim to keep everything square so that the joints don't cause the frame to twist.

27

The haunched mortise and tenon is ideal when making a frame that is grooved to accept a panel, as in a door. The haunch can help to strengthen the joint, but here it also fits and fills the exposed end of the groove in the stile. Where possible, make the groove the same size as the mortise and cut out the mortise as previously described, after first cutting the groove. (See page 101.)

Mark out the tenon and saw down the cheeks, but mark off and retain the haunch portion when sawing off the remaining waste. Trim to fit. **(27)**

28

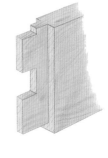

Double tenons are used when joining wide rails to stiles where the long mortise required for a single, wide tenon would weaken the stile, or where a wide tenon might become loose through shrinkage. It is, for example, the correct joint to use when jointing large panelled doors and deep apron table frames. Mark out the joint as shown above. Cut the mortise, including the recess for the tenon haunch and central tongue, first. Then mark out and cut the double tenon, haunch, and tongue. Trim to fit. **(28)**

There are machines for cutting mortises, as well as attachments that you can fit to a bench drill to do the same. Tenoning machines are used in commercial manufacture, but on a smaller scale, by using suitable jigs, you can cut tenons on a circular saw or band saw, or with a router.

29

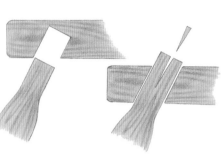

Blind socket   Through-and-wedged socket

30

Mark

Drill

Round tenons into drilled sockets This is the traditional joint often used in stool- and chair-making to join legs to seats or cross rails to uprights. Sockets can be either bored "through" or "blind"; through joints are often wedged **(29)**. Some woodworkers advocate tapered sockets, but straight, parallel-sided sockets give a more secure joint. First, bore out the required size of socket using a drill bit – the saw-toothed Forstner bit is most suitable – and then make the round tenon by whittling with a knife or rounding with cutting or abrasive tools. A general rule of thumb is that the socket depth should not be less than the socket diameter.

Draw boring (pegging joints) An old method of tightening up and securing mortise and tenon joints is to insert a wooden pin or peg through the joint. This is known as draw boring, and it is often incorrectly copied in some modern reproduction furniture by boring through the assembled joint and simply fitting a dowel.

The correct way of making this joint is as follows. After you have cut the joint, but with the tenon withdrawn, bore a suitable hole through the side of the mortise. Then replace the tenon to its full depth and insert the drill again to just mark the surface of the tenon inside the mortise. Withdraw the tenon, re-mark it about 1⁄16in (1.5mm) nearer to the shoulder and drill through at this point. The slight offset you have created will draw the joint up really tight when you drive the pin in. The pin should be straight grained and its head should be slightly larger than the hole and tapered to a point to ease starting. Cut the pin off flush on completion. **(30)**

Finishing

Some woods are more durable than others, but all will benefit from some kind of applied finish. Some finishes are designed to protect the surface by sealing the pores of the wood. Others, such as opaque paint, are used to obliterate or disguise the surface, while transparent polishes and varnishes serve to enhance and highlight the natural features of the wood. Additionally, finishes used on furniture act to give some resistance to the wear and tear of everyday use and abuse. Furthermore, many surface finishes can be renewed as time, and fashion, dictate.

Today there is a bewildering variety of wood-finishing materials. However, in earlier times, while there were several paint formulations and some oils and waxes, there was far less choice. For the country woodworker choice was further limited by both cost and availability.

The subject of finishes is a complex one and here it is possible to make only general comments. Your local paint dealer should be able to advise you, and always read the manufacturers' labels on proprietary products before making your choice.

PAINT

The painted furniture and artifacts of Ancient Egypt and the evidence of the use of colour in medieval dwellings give us some clues to the early use of "paint". Locally available earth and vegetable pigments were used to colour a suitable medium, such as water (to make limewash and distemper), or combinations of water and other ingredients, such as linseed oil and egg yolk (to make tempera). Linseed oil was also used to make oil paints.

Milk paint Limewash and distemper proved less suitable for use on wood than on walls, and egg tempera and oil paint are expensive and time-consuming to make. In due course a compromise product was found – milk paint. Milk paint is made by mixing earth pigments with skimmed milk and a little lime. In the rural communities of North America in particular, where its inexpensive ingredients were readily available and easy to prepare, milk paint became extremely popular. As well as being easy to apply, it dries to a durable, smooth, flat (matt) finish. Moreover, milk paint produces clear colours that mellow nicely with age.

You apply milk paint with a brush or sponge, and since it is water soluble it is pleasant to use and dries quite quickly, becoming lighter in colour as it does so. A second coat will increase the opacity of the finish. When the paint has dried you can add a clear lacquer, glaze, or wax to seal and darken the surface. Milk paint is an authentic "old" paint finish, and one that is also environmentally friendly. Modern water-soluble paints include a range of acrylics and emulsion paints.

Oil paint Oil-based paints were originally a mix of linseed oil, pigment, and white lead, with turpentine as a solvent. In modern formulations, oil-based paint is more likely to be a blend of oils and synthetic resins, with the lead omitted for health and safety reasons. The usual solvent is white spirit. Available in a very wide range of colours and three different finishes – matt, semigloss, and gloss – these paints are totally opaque and provide a reasonably tough and durable surface finish. However, with bare wood you first need to apply a primer or undercoat. The disadvantages of oil paint are that it is slow to dry and brushes and so on have to be cleaned in white spirit.

VARNISHES

Traditional varnish is made from natural gums, such as copal, dissolved in oil (linseed) or spirit (methylated). This produces a product with a transparent, or near transparent, appearance that you can apply to prepared bare wood or over matt paint to act as a protective top coat. Varnish also acts as a preservative and as a means of obtaining a good, hardwearing surface finish.

Today, the most common type of "varnish" is polyurethane, available in matt, semigloss (satin), and gloss. Polyurethane gives a hard, durable finish and it also provides effective protection against moisture. It is best to brush on a number of thinned coats (diluted half and half by volume with white spirit) than one full-strength application straight from the tin. Allow each coat to dry thoroughly and rub back the surface of each coat (except the final top coat) with very fine abrasive paper. Be meticulous about removing dust, though, or the surface finish will be marred.

STAINS

Wood stains alter or enrich the colour of wood and enhance the natural figure, or grain pattern, of a piece of furniture. There are four general types: water stains, spirit stains, oil stains, and chemical stains. Never use any stain without first testing it.

Prepare the wood carefully before staining it. Surface blemishes and coarse grain will be emphasized by the stain, while patches of grease or adhesive will reject the treatment and leave an uneven finish.

Water stains penetrate the fibres of the wood, but in so doing they cause the grain to rise, making it necessary to sand the wood smooth before proceeding. Wetting the wood with water, allowing it to dry, and then sanding before staining reduces this problem. Oil stains do not cause the grain to rise, but they are slow drying and relatively expensive. Spirit-based stains are probably the most difficult to apply evenly due to their rapid drying time – dark patches where the stain overlaps can be a problem. Chemical stains work by reacting with the wood and the resulting colour can be unpredictable. After applying any stain, and after it has thoroughly dried, seal the surface of the wood with a varnish, oil, or wax.

WAX AND OIL

Beeswax and linseed oil are probably the oldest known surface finishes. Both are transparent, or nearly so, and both impart a wonderful lustre that brings out the best qualities of colour and grain. Readily available and quite easy to apply, both are popular and well liked. The disadvantages of both are that they offer comparatively little surface protection and are easily marred. But the virtue of these finishes is that they are easy to renew.

Wax There are several good polishes you can buy, but make sure the one you choose is based on beeswax – some use paraffin wax instead. Avoid polishes that contain silicon – these produce the much advertised "sparkle", but not much else in terms of protecting or nourishing the wood. All waxes are incompatible with some finishes – paint, for example, won't adhere to wax.

You can apply a wax polish to bare wood and progressively build up the surface you want with additional applications. However, by giving the wood an initial application of a sealer, such as sanding sealer or a thinned coat of shellac or polyurethane, the wax will be more evenly distributed and you will save yourself a lot of work. Rub the sealer down with a very fine abrasive before waxing. Apply the wax with a soft cloth, rub it in well, and leave it to dry for a few minutes before buffing it with a clean, dry cloth. Subsequent applications of wax will improve the sheen and, in time, help to produce a rich patination.

Oil "Once a day for a week, once a week for a month, once a month for a year, and once a year forever" is an old adage about applying an oil finish. The traditional oil was linseed, and its use does indeed require numerous applications. Each must dry (by oxidization) before the next is applied, and the idea is to go on doing this until the wood can absorb no more oil.

Boiled linseed oil dries more quickly than the raw oil, but modern formulations, such as teak, tung, and Danish

oils incorporating rapid oxidizing agents, are now more commonly used. You apply these proprietary oils in the same way as linseed, by brushing or on a cloth, but because they are more penetrating and quicker to dry, they require only two or three applications.

AGEING

There are various techniques you can use to simulate the effects of age, sunlight, dust, damp, and the general wear and tear of years of use. Known generally as "distressing" or "antiquing", these methods are now widely practised and accepted for their aesthetic appeal, although they are also used by fakers trying to pass modern-built furniture off as genuinely old. Distressing can involve doing actual damage to the wood, as well as using special finishes to simulate fading, peeling, crazing, patination, and similar effects.

Distressing wood

Before applying any finish, you can artificially age wood by denting or scratching it, by scrubbing its surface with a wire brush, and by rounding over or purposely chipping corners and edges. Softwoods such as pine are especially suited to the wire-brush method. Wear on chair rails, table legs, and so on can easily be simulated by abrading these surfaces; for an authentic look, make sure that you apply this artificially induced damage where it would be most likely to occur in normal use.

A common method of further ageing new wood is to wipe it over with an antiquing glaze, made by mixing together small amounts of pigment such as burnt umber, raw sienna, or Vandyke brown in a transparent oil glaze. Make up a suitable glaze by mixing 1 part boiled linseed oil with 2 parts white spirit, or substitute thinned oil, varnish, or polyurethane. Alternatively, you can use a water-based glaze. Simply wipe or brush on this tinted glaze and then immediately wipe it off again, leaving pigment behind in the dents, hollows, and cracks.

Thinned grey or cream matt-finish paint brushed on and wiped off again will leave enough pigment behind in the grain of hardwoods to simulate age or a limewashed effect. Proprietary "old pine" stain will also convincingly age softwoods. Formulations containing lime, caustic

soda, ammonia, or sulphuric acid can also be effective, but they are dangerous to use and you need to take extreme care.

Antique waxes – wax polish containing darkening pigments – applied to new wood will quickly give the appearance of a build-up of polish and dirt, which is what gives the patina of age. You can buy suitable wax polishes ready tinted, or make them up yourself by adding pigments or shoe polish to ordinary wax furniture polish.

Distressing paint

You can also apply antiquing glaze over a painted surface. This will darken the colour of the paint, producing an effect that would naturally take years to achieve. Rubbing a painted surface with abrasive paper or wire wool will lighten its colour, simulating both wear and tear and the effects of exposure to sunlight. Abrading the surface colour right off in places will allow underlying paint colours to show through in those areas. This can be a very effective technique. You can also try applying a first coat of paint, allowing it to dry before applying a second one in a contrasting colour, and before this second coat has dried, rub it off in the areas that would normally receive the most wear to reveal the colour beneath (and perhaps, too, some areas of bare wood). It is very helpful to examine a real antique painted piece first to give you some ideas of how the end result should look.

Flaking paint is often a characteristic associated with old furniture, especially items that have been exposed to damp. Applying patches of wax, either to bare wood or a previously painted surface, will stop additional coats of paint adhering to those patches. When the top coat is dry, gently rub back the previously waxed areas to cause the paint to flake. Dampness may also cause painted surfaces to crack and craze. You can simulate this by using special "crackle" varnishes. This process makes use of the incompatibility and different drying times of oil-based and water-based varnishes. The best effects are achieved when two coats of contrasting base paints are used. If required, you can wipe more colour into the cracked surface after it has dried.

All distressing and antiquing processes require careful application if they are to be convincing. Bear in mind that wear would occur in some areas more than others, and that dust and dirt tends to accumulate in recesses such as deep mouldings. Also bear in mind that exposed surfaces, such as sharp edges, table tops, and drawer fronts, would tend to be lighter in colour due to wear and the fading effects of sunlight. Around door and drawer handles you would also find signs of wear and tear and a build-up of grime. Use artists' colours applied with a small brush to produce the desired effect.

Once you have achieved an aged appearance, apply a protective coat of varnish – but don't let it get too shiny.

The brightly coloured boxes on page 108 reveal a definite eye for colour and an appreciation of timeless beauty as well as usefulness.

The simple but solid construction of the two-tier cupboard on page 109, with its well-worn paint finish, is typical of what has become known as the "New England" style – although I suspect it owes a lot to an old English style. Its appearance is perhaps due to many years of over painting, layer upon layer as the years went by. Alternatively, the effect may be totally artificial, achieved by judicious application of layers of paint then rubbed through and "distressed", as described above, to give that well used look. The ladder-back, rush-seated chair in the same picture has been painted with a matt earth red and subsequently waxed to impart a desirable deep sheen to its surface.

Various painted artifacts are displayed on a decidedly rustic table or bench (left) finished with a shiny gloss varnish on bare wood.

Wood Guide

It helps to know something of a wood's characteristics – its working properties, colour, durability, and so on – before choosing a particular type for a project. It also helps to know if it is botanically a hardwood (H) or a softwood (S). On the following pages you will find a brief guide to those North American and European timbers that have been used or recommended for the projects contained in this book, and that are easily available to the country woodworker.

You can readily purchase prepared wood from timber yards and other retail outlets (see Directory, pages 124–5). Softwoods are generally less expensive to buy than hardwoods, but are also less durable. In some countries, large quantities of wood, both hardwoods and softwoods, are sold by volume – i.e. by the cubic foot. This is a quantity of wood equal to a board 1in thick x 12in wide x 12ft long (25mm x 305mm x 3.6m). For smaller quantities of wood it is more usual to be quoted a price per piece or per foot (or metre) for a given, measured section. The standard measurement in America is the board foot, which is equal to a board 1in thick x 12in square (25mm x 305mm square).

The characteristic birch of North America is the paper birch (*Betula papyrifera*).

ASH (H)

The European ash (*Fraxinus excelsior*) is a large tree whose common name generally reflects its origins. In Canada and the United States, the ash (*F. americana*) is generally a little smaller, but there are many varieties, such as black, white, yellow, and blue ash. It has a coarse but usually straight grain and is characterized by its strength and resilience. It is whitish to light brown in colour, has a distinctive figure (grain pattern), is easy to work, and takes a good polish. However, it is not durable outdoors unless it is treated with a suitable preservative.

BEECH (H)

This strong, hardwearing wood has good working properties. The European beech (*Fagus sylvatica*) grows into a large tree and is favoured for its fine, uniform texture. The American beech (*F. grandifolia*) is a relatively small tree but with similar strength and working properties to its European counterpart, although it does have a slightly coarser texture. Beech is generally pale to reddish-brown in colour, and although its figure often lacks character, it stains and polishes well. It requires treatment with a preservative if you intend to use it in damp conditions.

BIRCH (H)

This is probably the world's hardiest and most widespread tree. Birch (*Betula sp.*) varies from invasive scrub to moderate-sized trees. The characteristic birch of North America is the paper birch (*B. papyrifera* – shown on page 114), while sweet birch (*B. lenta*) and yellow birch (*B. alleghanensis*) are also common. In Britain, the silver birch (*B. pendula*) and *B. pubescens* are common. Birch has a creamy white sap wood and pale brown heartwood. It works and finishes reasonably well but it is not durable when used outdoors.

CEDAR (S)

The true cedar, cedar of Lebanon (*Cedrus libani*), is a large tree with a trunk up to 5ft (1.5m) in diameter. Its wood is straight grained if a little brittle, but it is easy to work (except around any knots). The cedar has an aromatic wood whose scent discourages moths. American "cedars" include white cedar (*Thuja occidentalis*), western red cedar (*T. plicata*), yellow cedar (*Chamaecyparis nootkatensis*), and others. Both the white and western red cedar are reddish brown in colour and slightly coarse grained, and western red cedar splits easily. Yellow cedar is fine textured, easily worked, and pale yellow in colour.

CHERRY (H)

American cherry, also known as black cherry (*Prunus serotina*), is a good, decorative wood, fine textured and straight grained. It makes a tree of moderate size, although there are smaller varieties such as the pin and sweet cherries. The European cherry (*P. avium*) is also a small tree and its wood is mainly used only for small-scale work. Cherry wood, which is reddish-brown in colour, is not difficult to work if your tools are sharp. It finishes well and takes a high polish.

ELM (H)

Once common in parts of North America and Britain, elm – including *Ulmus americana* and *U. procera*, the American and English elms, respectively – is fast disappearing due to the ravages of Dutch elm disease. Larger in size in Britain than in America, elm trees produce wood that is coarse-textured and often cross-grained, but it works well when sharp tools are used. Its colour is beige-brown and most varieties and hybrids have an attractive figure, especially *U. procera*. It is not naturally durable when used outdoors.

HAZEL (H)

More of a shrub than a tree, the European hazel (*Corylus avellana*) is widespread throughout much of Britain where, in the past, it was extensively grown as coppice. It produces strong, straight sticks for a variety of craft applications. Native American hazels include *C. americana* and *C. californica*.

HICKORY (H)

Native to Canada and eastern parts of America, hickory (*Carya glabra*, *C. laciniosa*, among others) is a strong, straight-grained wood similar in appearance and main characteristics to ash. However, its fibrous wood is tougher than that of ash.

LIME (H)

A fine-textured wood, lime (*Tilia vulgaris*), also known as linden, is easily worked and, because it cuts evenly in all directions, is excellent when you want a wood for carving. It has a creamy white coloured wood. The American lime (*T. americana*) is known as Basswood – the name that is also given to the wood of the tulip tree.

MAPLE (H)

Of the many maples, sugar maple (*Acer saccharum*), also known as hard or rock maple, is perhaps best known throughout North America. It is a heavy, hard wood with a close-textured grain, white to pale brown in colour. It can sometimes be difficult to work, but it is hard-wearing and finishes well. Red maple (*A. rubrum*) is not as hard or strong as *Acer saccharum*, but it is easier to work. In Britain, the field maple (*A. campestre*) is generally little more than a small hedgerow tree of limited commercial value. None of the maples is naturally durable when used outdoors.

OAK (H)

There are many different oaks. American varieties are generally grouped as white oak (*Quercus alba*) and red oak (*Q. rubra*), while the two varieties native to Britain are the common, or European, oak (*Q. robur*) and the sessile oak (*Q. petraea*). Oak wood is renowned for its strength and durability, but these qualities vary according to growing conditions and growth rates. All are hard and durable and work well. White oak has similar characteristics to the European varieties, while red oak is coarser grained and has a less attractive figure. Colour varies from pale yellow to brown, often with a pinkish tint. Oak wood contains tannic acid, which corrodes ferrous metals.

PINE (S)

This wood is probably used more than any other. Pine is the general name given to all members of the *Pinus* family – and, commercially, to several others that are not. The character of the 35 or so varieties of American pine varies geographically from the hard pitch pines of the south (*P. palustris*) to the softer pines, such as Weymouth or yellow pine (*P. strobus*) of the east, and the western white pine (*P. monticola*). Yellow pine is an easily worked wood, pale yellow to brown in colour, while western white pine is similar in appearance but tougher. In Europe, Scots pine (*P. sylvestris*), especially, provides the popular red deal or redwood, which is a relatively strong, slightly resinous wood, yellow-brown to red-brown in colour, often with a distinctive figure. It works easily and well (except around the knots), and can be brought to a good finish. All the varieties of pines take stain, paint, and polish well. However, none is durable outdoors unless first treated with a suitable preservative.

SYCAMORE (H)

American and British sycamores are unrelated trees – the former belong to the plane family (*Platanus occidentalis*), while the latter are maples (*Acer pseudoplatanus*), the false plane. The American sycamore is an even-textured wood, pale reddish-brown in colour. It is easy to work and polishes well. The British sycamore also has an even texture, but it is finer textured than its American equivalent, and is white to creamy white in colour. It works and finishes well, coming to a lustrous surface. However, neither species is durable if used outdoors.

WALNUT (H)

This is a distinctive wood with some excellent characteristics. American black walnut (*Juglans nigra*) is a large tree. It has a tough, rather coarse-textured wood, with both straight and wavy grain. Its heartwood is rich purple-brown to black in colour. It works well, takes a high polish, and is moderately durable outdoors. European walnut (*J. regia*) is a smaller tree, and its wood varies in colour from grey brown to brown, often with darker streaks. Its characteristics and working properties are similar to *J. nigra*.

Templates

These template patterns have been grouped together by project. To save space the patterns overlap, but the pieces are distinguished by the differently shaped "bubbles" along one of the edges of each template, showing which project it belongs to (see the key on the right). Make a separate tracing for each pattern piece, labelling each one. The templates on pages 118–22 are shown at 80 per cent of the required size, and those on page 123 are at c.25 per cent. The former can be enlarged on a photocopier at 125 per cent, but you will probably have to scale up the latter with a grid (see page 123).

♡ **Duck Decoy** 6 patterns, page 119
▽ **Cutting Boards** 2 patterns (B & C), pages 118, 119
▽ **Spoon Rack** 2 patterns, page 118
◇ **Candle Box** 3 patterns, page 120
⬡ **Five-Board Bench** 1 pattern, page 120
⬡ **Hooded Cradle** 2 patterns, page 121
☐ **Folk Bed** 1 pattern, page 121
○ **Traditional Whirligig** 8 patterns, page 122
◇ **Rocking Chair** 5 patterns, page 123
◯ **Shaker Shelves** 1 pattern, page 123

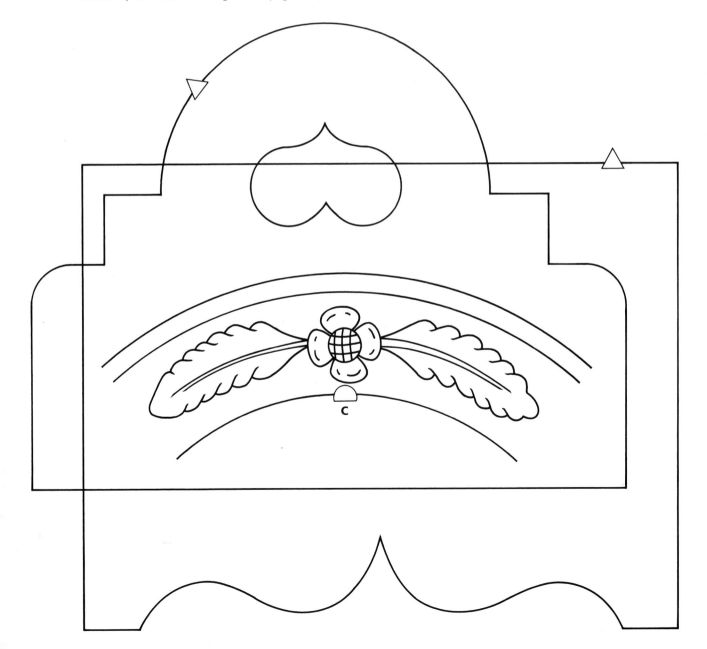

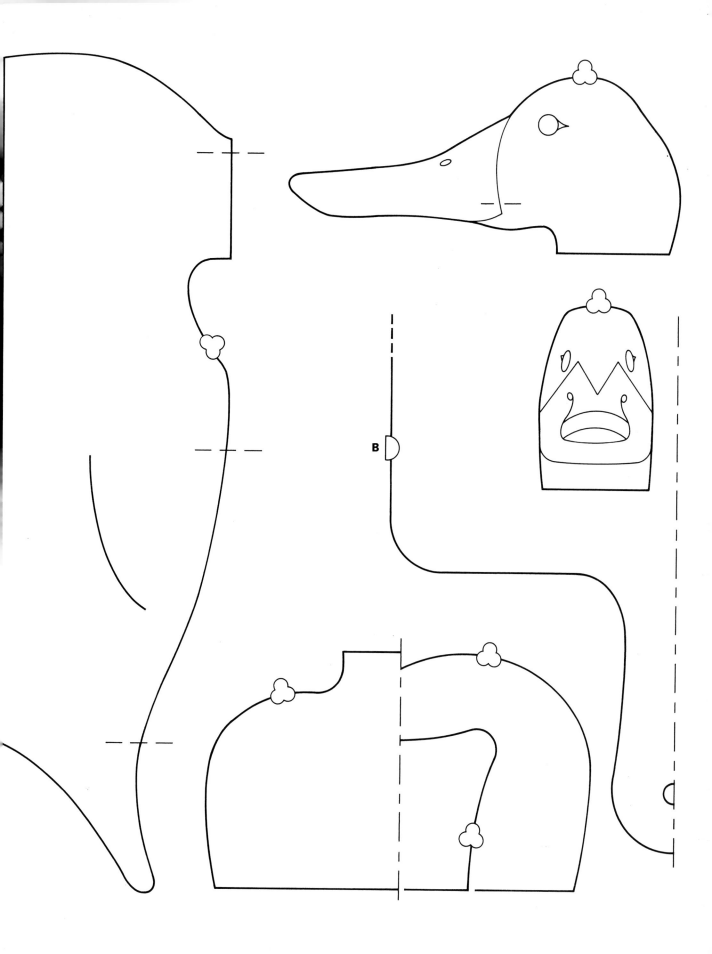

B

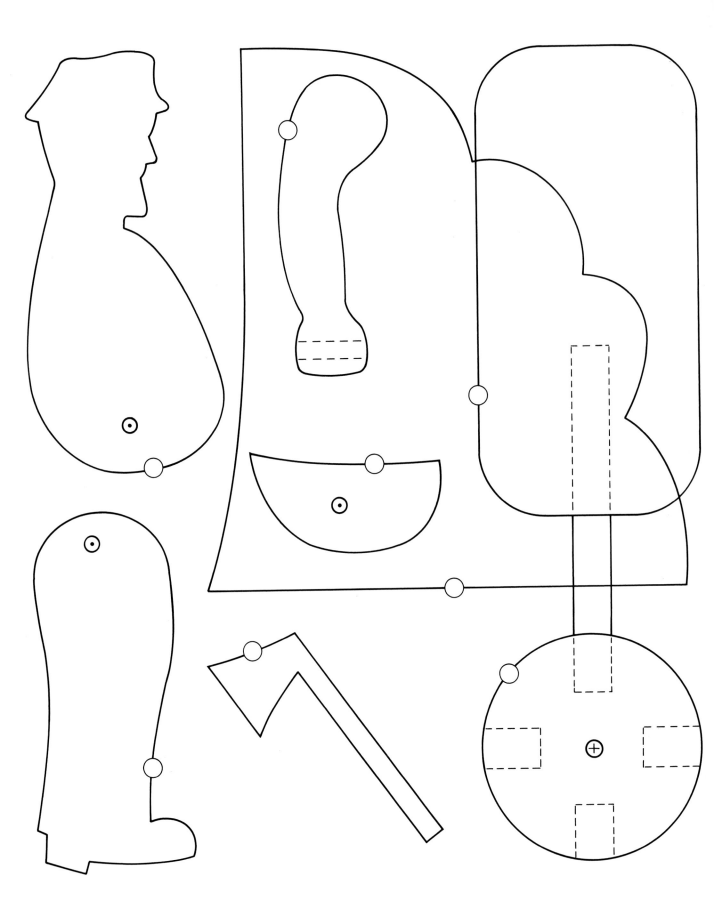

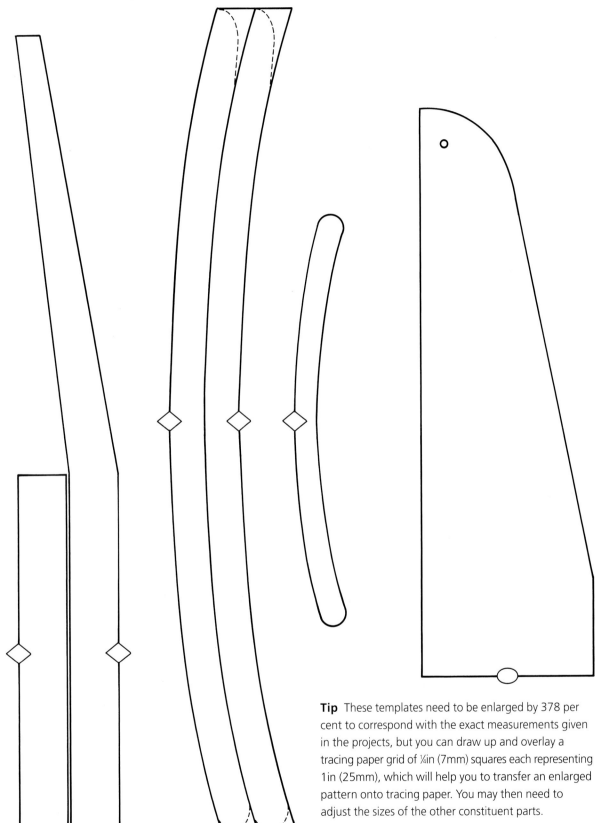

Tip These templates need to be enlarged by 378 per cent to correspond with the exact measurements given in the projects, but you can draw up and overlay a tracing paper grid of ¼in (7mm) squares each representing 1in (25mm), which will help you to transfer an enlarged pattern onto tracing paper. You may then need to adjust the sizes of the other constituent parts.

Directory of Suppliers

Note: while every effort has been made to ensure that the following details are accurate and up-to-date, they may vary from time to time. Contact to confirm opening times before visiting. (Don't forget the "www." prefix for websites.)

WOOD AND TOOLS

BRITAIN

British Gates & Timber Ltd
Castletons Oak Sawmills
Biddenden, Ashford
Kent TN27 8DD
britishgates.co.uk
Tel +44 (0)1580 291555
Wood, tools, accessories.

Craft Supplies Limited
The Mill, Millers Dale, Buxton
Derbyshire SK17 8SN
Tel +44 (0)1298 871636
craft-supplies.co.uk
Wood, tools, accessories, finishing supplies.

Fine Wood & Tool Store
Riverside Sawmills
Boroughbridge
North Yorkshire YO5 9LJ
Tel +44 (0)1423 322370
Hardwoods, tools, books, finishing supplies.

Limehouse Timber Ltd
18 Robert Leonard Ind. Estate
Stock Road, Southend-on-Sea
Essex SS2 5QD
Tel +44 (0)1702 469292
Native & imported hardwoods.

W.L. West & Sons Ltd
Salham, Petworth
West Sussex GU28 0PU
Tel +44 (0)1798 861611
wlwest.co.uk
Native & imported hardwoods & softwoods.

Yandle & Sons Ltd
Hurst Works, Martock
Somerset TA12 6JU
Tel +44 (0)1935 822207
yandle.co.uk
Wood, tools, accessories.

USA

Colonial Hardwoods Inc.
7953 Cameron Brown Ct
Springfield, VA 22153
Toll-free +1 800 466 5451
colonialhardwoods.com
Domestic hardwoods.

Constantines Wood Center
1040 East Oakland Park Blvd
Fort Lauderdale, FL 33334
Toll-free +1 800 443 9667
www.constantines.com
Wood, tools, related supplies.

Craft Supplies USA
PO Box 50300
Provo, UT 84605-0030
Toll-free +1 800 551 8876
woodturnerscatalog.com
Tools, accessories.

Garrett Wade Co., Inc.
161 Avenue of the Americas
New York, NY 100313
Toll-free +1 800 221 2942
garrettwade.com
Wood, tools, related supplies.

Handloggers
305 Cutting Blvd
Port Richmond, CA 94804
Toll-free +1 800 461 1969
handloggers.com
Hardwoods.

Talarico Hardwoods
22 Hardwood Lane
Mohnton, PA 19540-9939
Tel +1 (610) 775 0400
talaricohardwoods.com
Domestic hardwoods.

Willard Brothers
300 Basin Road
Trenton, NJ 08619
Toll-free +1 800 320 6519
willardbrothers.net
Domestic hardwoods.

Woodcraft
560 Airport Industrial Park
PO Box 1686, Parkersburg
WV 26102-1686
Toll-free +1 800 225 1153
woodcraft.com
Wood, tools, accessories.
Call/check website for stores.

Woodcrafter's Supply
7703 Perry Highway (Rte 19)
Pittsburgh, PA 15237
Tel +1 (412) 367 4330
woodcrafterssupply.com
Domestic & imported wood, tools, books.

PAINTS AND FINISHES

BRITAIN

Craig & Rose plc
Unit 8, Halbeath Ind. Estate
Crossgates Road
Dunfermline, Fife KY11 7EG
Tel +44 (0)1383 740011
craigandrose.com
Traditional varnishes.

Farrow & Ball Ltd
Uddens Trading Estate
Wimborne, Dorset BH21 7NL
Tel +44 (0)1202 876141
farrow-ball.com
Traditional paints.

Liberon
Mountfield Industrial Estate
New Romney, Kent TN28 8XU
Tel +44 (0)1797 367555
Finishing products.

Pine Brush Products / Colourman
The Bowjy, Trevowhan
Morvah, Pendeen
Penzance, Cornwall TR20 8YT
Tel +44 (0)1736 787420
Milk paint & other finishing products, brushes.

Rustins Ltd
Waterloo Rd, Lon NW2 7TX
Tel +44 (0)20 8450 4666
rustins.co.uk
Finishing & restoration products.

Stencil Bazaar
Heart of the Country Village

Swinsen, Nr Litchfield
Staffordshire WS14 9QR
Tel/Fax +44 (0)1543 480669
heartofthecountryvillage.co.uk
American traditional paints.

USA

**The Old Fashioned Milk
Paint Co., Inc.**
436 Main Street
Groton, MA 01450
Tel +1 (978) 448 6336
milkpaint.com
Historic natural milk paints.

Flax Art & Design
1699 Market Street
San Francisco, CA 94103
Tel +1 (415) 552 2355
flaxart.com
Paint products.

Martin Senour Paints
101 Prospect Ave. NW
Cleveland, OH 44115
Toll-free +1 800 677 5270
martinsenour.com
*Paint products. Call/check
website for dealers.*

Wood Finish Supply
PO Box 929
Fort Bragg, CA 95437
Toll-free +1 800 245 5611
finishsupply.com
Finishing products.

MISCELLANEOUS

BRITAIN
Jacobs, Young & Westbury
Bridge Road, Haywards Heath

West Sussex RH16 1UA
Tel +44 (0)1444 412411
*Seat weaving materials,
rush cane & cord.*

H.E. Savill
9–12 St Martin's Place
Scarborough
North Yorkshire YO11 2QH
Tel +44 (0)1723 373032
Period furniture fittings.

Shaker Shop
49 Lambs Conduit Street
London WC1N 3NG
Tel +44 (0)845 331 2055
shaker.co.uk
(also based in Gloucestershire)
*Shaker furniture, pegs, kits,
seating tape.*

Woodfit Ltd
Kern Mill, Whittle-le-Woods
Chorley, Lancashire PR6 7EA
Tel +44 (0)1257 266421
woodfit.com
*Traditional & modern
furniture hardware.*

USA
Ball & Ball
463 West Lincoln Highway
Exton, PA 19341-2705
Toll-free +1 800 257 3711
ballandball-us.com
*Furniture hardware
reproductions & restorations*

Connecticut Cane & Reed
PO Box 762
Manchester, CT 06045
Toll-free +1 800 241 9741

caneandreed.com
*Seat-weaving materials,
Shaker seating tape.*

The Hardware Division, LLC
600 High Street
Naugatuck, CT 06770
Toll-free +1 866 837 1969
wayneswoods.com
*Reproduction knobs & poles
in wood, brass, & glass.*

Howard Kaplan Antiques
827 Broadway
New York, NY 10003
Tel +1 (212) 674 1000
howardkaplanantiques.com
Country-style furniture.

Paxton Hardware Ltd
PO Box 256
Upper Falls MD 21156
Toll-free +1 800 241 9741
paxtonhardware.com
Locks, hinges, etc.

Shaker Workshops
14 South Pleasant Street
PO Box 8001, Ashburnham
MA 01430-8001
Toll-free +1 800 840 9121
shakerworkshops.com
Shaker furniture, kits, etc

PLACES OF INTEREST

BRITAIN
American Museum in Britain
Claverton Manor
Bath, Avon BA2 7BD
Tel +44 (0)1225 460503
americanmuseum.org

*Colonial & Shaker interiors,
furniture & artifacts.*

Highland Folk Museum
Duke Street, Kingussie
Inverness-shire PH21 1JG
Tel +44 (0)1540 661307
highlandfolk.com
Early local furniture & artifacts.

Museum of Lakeland Life
Abbot Hall
Kendal, Cumbria LA9 5AL
Tel +44 (0)1539 722464
lakelandmuseum.org.uk
*Trade workshops & period
interiors, furniture, artifacts,
tools, etc.*

**Norfolk Rural Life Museum
(Roots of Norfolk)**
Gressenhall
Dereham, Norfolk NR20 4DR
Tel +44 (0)1362 860563
museums.norfolk.gov.uk
Labourers' cottage & artifacts.

Museum of Welsh Life
St Fagans, Cardiff CF5 6XB
Tel +44 (0)29 2057 3500
nmgw.ac.uk/mwl
*Furnished period cottages,
rural artifacts, tools.*

**Weald and Downland
Open Air Museum**
Singleton, Chichester
West Sussex PO18 0EU
Tel +44 (0)1243 811363
wealddown.co.uk
*Traditional buildings,
furniture, & artifacts.*

USA

Adirondack Museum
PO Box 99, Blue Mountain Lake
NY 12812-0099
Tel +1 (518) 352 7311
adirondackmuseum.org
Regional crafts & furniture.

Colonial Williamsburg
PO Box 1776, Williamsburg
VA 23187-1776
Tel +1 (757) 229 1000
history.org
Colonial interiors & artifacts.

Hancock Shaker Village
Albany Road, Route 20
PO Box 927
Pittsfield, MA 02102
Tel +1 (413) 443 0188
hancockshakervillage.org
Shaker interiors, artifacts, etc.

Met. Museum of Art
1000 5th Avenue at 82nd St
New York, NY 10028-0198
Tel +1 (212) 535 7710
metmuseum.org
Early furniture & artifacts.

Old Sturbridge Village
1 Old Sturbridge Village Road
Sturbridge, MA 01566
Tel +1 (508) 347 3362
osv.org
Colonial furniture & artifacts.

Winterthur Museum
Winterthur, Route 52
Winterthur, DE 19735
Tel +1 800 448 3883
winterthur.org
*Period American
& English furniture.*

WOODWORKING COURSES

BRITAIN
Chris Mowe
(See Colourman, page 124)
Antique paint finishing.

West Dean College
West Dean, Chichester
West Sussex PO18 0QZ
Tel +44 (0)1243 811301
westdean.org.uk
*Furniture-making, chair-seat
weaving, finishing.*

USA

Anderson Ranch
5263 Owl Creek Road
Snowmass, CO 81615
Tel +1 (970) 923 3181
andersonranch.org
Various woodworking courses.

John C. Campbell Folk Sch
1 Folk School Road
Brasstown, NC 28902-9603
Toll-free +1 800 365 5724
folkschool.com
Folk arts & crafts.

Country Workshops
990 Black Pine Ridge Road
Marshall, NC 28753
Tel +1 828 656 2280
countryworkshops.org
*Country & green
woodworking.*

**Dana Robes Wood
Craftsmen**
Rte 4A, Lower Shaker Village
Enfield, NH 03748
Toll-free +1 800 722 5036
danarobes.com
Shaker furniture & artifacts.

**Connecticut Valley School
of Woodworking**
(Mario Rodriguez)
249 Spencer St.
Manchester, CT 06040
Tel +1 860-647-0303
schoolofwoodworking.com
*Various woodworking
courses.*

Bibliography

Gilborn, Craig. *Adirondack
Furniture and the Rustic
Tradition,* Abrams Inc., New
York. 1987.

Hill, Jack. *Country Chair
Making.* David & Charles,
Newton Abbot. 1993.

Hill, Jack. *Jack Hill's
Country Furniture.* Cassell
Illustrated, London. 1998.

Kettell, Russell H. *The Pine
Furniture of Early New England.*
Dover, New York. 1949.

Kinmonth, Claudia.
Irish Country Furniture.
Yale University Press. 1993.

Knell, David. *English
Country Furniture.*
Berry & Jenkins,
London. 1992.

Mack, Daniel. *Making
Rustic Furniture.* Sterling
Lark, New York. 1992.

Miller, Judith & Martin.
Period Finishes and Effects.
Mitchell Beazley, London. 1992.

Shea, John G. *Antique
Country Furniture of North
America.* Van Nostrand
Reinhold, New York. 1975.

Sparkes, Ivan. *English
Domestic Furniture.*
Spurbooks, Bourne
End. 1980.

Sprigg, J. & Larkin, D.
Shaker: Life, Work, and Art.
Cassell, London. 1988.

Index

Acknowledgments

I thank the publishers, Mitchell Beazley, for allowing me to revisit *Country Woodworker* in this new, re-worked, and abridged format. Sincere thanks are of course given to those directly involved in its editing, design, production, marketing, and distribution.

Thanks also to those involved in the creation of the original book: to James Merrell who was responsible for the photography; my American friends, Merryll and Ed Saylan, who read parts of the manuscript, and Chris Mowe and Henryk Terpilowski for advice on antique finishing.

Finally, I wish to thank all those who, over the years (three score and ten already!), have taught me to love and understand wood and how to make useful things with it. And I thank God for the trees we all use.

The publisher would like to thank the following for kindly allowing us to photograph their homes for the original book: Shirley Dupree, Fran Sansom and Jack Hill, Howard Kaplan, Tasha and Jack Polizzi, George Schmidt, Maryanne Wilkins.